In my years of leader to partner with great leaders and mentor aspiring leaders. Often, these aspiring leaders are looking for the secret to success. *Stop Clowning Around* demonstrates the secret by breaking down the ten essential skillsets that will lead to professional success. The secret of course is taking care of the people. Customers and employees are the lifeblood of any organization. When professionals master these essentials and learn to care for the people, career success is in their future.

— JAMIE HAENGGI, CHIEF CUSTOMER
OFFICER, ADT

The world is continuously changing. If we've learned anything about life in 2020, it's that a "new normal" is always just around the corner.

But at the same time, while external circumstances are never the same from one moment to the next, let alone from one generation to the next, people of all ages are always hoping and dreaming of achieving the same things:

- Success in their personal lives,

- Success in their professional lives,

- Greater recognition,

- Greater accomplishment and achievement,

- Etc … (insert your own biggest goals here).

It stands to reason then that there are things we can learn from people who have achieved those goals. This is true about the young person just starting on their journey to make their mark in the world. It is also true about the seasoned adult wanting to change things up and level up from wherever they are.

Scott Holman is someone who has achieved notable success. Not only did he start where many young people start, namely in a place of not being all that serious, but he also reached his success by following time-honored principles that he gleaned from other successful people. He has distilled those principles into ten essentials that we can use as a simple guideline for our own lives.

The bottom line here is that you don't need to read thousands of books to figure out your path forward. Just a few good ones like *Stop Clowning Around* by Scott Holman.

— JEFF CHEEK, VP OF LEARNING, NEW
HORIZONS LEARNING GROUP

STOP CLOWNING AROUND

SCOTT HOLMAN

CONTENTS

ISBN: 978-1-950566-16-7

Cover Design: Hackntog Design

Subjects: Personal growth, professional success, skills gap, soft skills, personal development, continuing education, career advancement.

To all the aspiring professionals struggling to find and navigate your way, keep learning, keep growing, and keep persevering.

Regardless of your start or the obstacles that get in your way, remember it is your show and it is worth mastering.

Stop Clowning Around!

.

For you created my inmost being; you knit me
together in my mother's womb.
I praise you because I am fearfully and wonderfully
made; your works are wonderful, I know that full
well.

— PSALM 139:13-14

FOREWORD

A survey of Fortune 500 CEO's not too long ago, found that 75% of long-term career success depends upon one's ability to develop soft skills.[1]

Based on a multitude of job listings and customer feedback, Jeff Weiner, CEO of LinkedIn, says that the number one skills gap in corporations today is soft skills. If anyone is in a position to judge what it is that companies are looking for in new hires, it would be the CEO of LinkedIn, far and away the leading job networking platform today.

So what are these soft skills that job offerers want so much to find in their employees? Apparently, they are a *relational* skill set, one that focuses on productive interactions between people. These relational skills are the skills most sought after by corporations all around the world. They may be called "soft skills," but their impact on one's life and surroundings are anything but soft!

Why are they even called "soft skills" one might ask. When Scott sent me the rough manuscript for this book, I *did* ask and did a little extracurricular research. I had heard of soft skills of course, but I always had sort of vaguely assumed that soft skills were skills you learned in life, and that hard skills were the skills God gave you when he designed you. Maybe it's because I equated hard and soft "skills" with hard and soft "ware" in the tech universe. It made sense to me that hard skills were like hardware. Your specs were your specs. But soft skills, like software, could make use of those specs in unforeseen and creative ways to make them sing. I had forged a nifty concept, but it wasn't exactly the right one.

It turns out that "soft skills" is a term initially used by the military. According to my online research, the U.S. military began studying leadership and performance back in the late 1960s. They needed to differentiate between skillsets their soldiers acquired, so they created two simple categories of skills. Hard skills were the skills needed to work with things that were hard (no kidding), like metal machinery. Soft skills were the skills necessary to work with things that were soft to the touch. The military struggled with these categories, though. Initially, skills that dealt with paper, so long as they were for the purpose of operating machines, were classified as hard skills. But skills that used paper but were not for the purpose of operating machines, were classified as soft skills. Fast forward some forty-odd years, and the term has survived, although nearly no one knows that the military first coined it. As we understand them today, soft skills are "people skills." Some call them EQ for "emotional intelligence quotient" (as in IQ for emotions). Others call them "super skills" or "power skills."

The point is that these skills are not as obvious, but every bit as important as all the other types of skills we work to acquire. They can dramatically impact a person's level of achievement in life. All too often, they are skills one only learns by experience and significantly acquires late in life. Sayings like "hindsight is 20-20" are an expression of this reality.

This book represents a treasure trove of soft/power/super skills knowledge to anyone who will read it and pay attention. The best thing about it is that it's not complicated or hard to understand. Scott has made it easy to take in. He's filled it with interesting quotes from famous accomplished people, and anecdotes and stories from his own life. He's even created a simplified matrix to build all his content around because he knows that people tend to remember better when knowledge is anchored to a matrix.

Read this book if you're young, and you'll avoid years of wasted time. Read this book if you're old, and you'll find yourself feeling young again and full of hope. Wherever you are in life, this book will inspire you and motivate you to get up tomorrow and do better at whatever it is that you most love to do.

— STEVE SCHOENHOFF, J.D., CO-FOUNDER &

CEO, KLUG PUBLISHING

DESPERATION OR DESTINY?

The only person you are destined to become is the
person you decide to be.

— RALPH WALDO EMERSON

Today Is Decision Day...

Today is the day that marks your path and sets you up for a
bright future. Today is the day that you decide to become the
person that you were always meant to be. The person who
brings clarity to critical conversations and insight to
outrageous problems. The person who lightens the workload
of their team and builds caring relationships with clients.
The person who remains unflappable in the face of office

chaos and flexible in an environment of ever-changing expectations. The person who stays curious about the world around them and influences company culture. (This is the opposite of being the office clown...but more on that later...)

This amazing, high-energy, self-aware, team-focused, empathetic, problem-solver is you!

This is you, because today is the day you are deciding that you are going to stop clowning around. Instead of heading into work and doing the same thing you have always done, you are making a foundational shift in your outlook. Instead of making the same choices, having the same reactions, and living your life in survival mode, you are going to reach for new thought processes, learn new skills, and take powerful steps to develop your mind, your actions, and ultimately, your life.

Where Are You At?

You might have picked up this book because you are tired of your dead-end job. You had big dreams when you started this job, but now you would just like to escape. You come home from work only to collapse on the couch in front of the television with a bag of chips. The thought of going into work tomorrow fills you with dread. The highlight of your workday is your ten-minute break that you try to stretch into fifteen, just so you can lift your spirits with cute puppy videos. You don't want to rehash the weird conversation that you had with your supervisor about your problematic co-worker. You are tired of the ever-changing office culture, the endless problems, and the staff turnover. You see possible fixes for the problems you are observing but aren't sure you will be heard when you have your next one-on-one with your direct report.

You know you have more to offer. You are bright, thoughtful, and articulate. But you are also exhausted and worn out. You need a new plan of action, or you won't make it another day, let alone another year. How can you turn this job around?

This book is for you.

Maybe you have been working in the same company for the last three years. You have passion and ideas to share, but you are having trouble communicating with your higher-ups. (Nervous sweats, anyone?) Come to think of it, you struggle communicating with your co-workers, too. (Talking is not your strong suit. If only they could read your mind.) You know that you have the technical abilities to get the job done, but somehow you keep hitting a wall when you share your vision with your team.

You are frustrated and doubting yourself. Maybe you don't have what it takes to keep building out your career. Maybe you will always be stuck in a mid-level position. But you have a sense in your gut that you could be more. Your frustration has led you to this moment in time. How do you achieve all that you know you are capable of?

This book is for you.

Maybe you are fresh out of grad school with your MBA tucked neatly in your pocket. You've got the brains, the determination, and the will to take the business world by storm. You found an entry-level job with the marketing division of an up and coming tech company but recognize you haven't quite found your niche. In fact, as you have been applying yourself (utilizing the thousands of dollars of education that you invested in yourself), you are finding that your natural gifts lie in sales (not marketing, which was the focus of your studies).

As you overhear the conversations on the sales floor, you have a million different ideas about how you can help the people on the phone. You love the thrill of the pitch. You are drawn to the collaborative nature of client management, but you are not quite sure how to get there. You just know that if you have to sit through one more lead generation brainstorming session, you might throw up. You want to get in on the action, not just lay out the battle plan.

How do you tell your boss that you would like to move to a different department...three months after being on the job? The workplace is revealing something you never knew about yourself. You are recognizing your strengths and want to figure out how to bring them into play. *How do you become a leader in an area that you didn't train for?*

This book is for you.

Or maybe your career journey sounds more like mine. You hated high school core classes (I carried my pillow to class with me senior year and slept on my desk), saw no real benefit to geometry (proofs are my nemesis), and are a college drop-out. You always thought you would have a job that you loved. You are creative, upbeat, and drawn to helping others, but can't seem to find a career to match your skill set.

To your amazement (and chagrin), no golden gates of opportunity have swung open to you. Your ideals of getting a perfect job have given way to the reality of being able to make ends meet. You have tried a wide variety of low paying jobs. (My resume includes pizza delivery guy, forklift driver, and detergent mixer). No matter what job you try, you just can't find the right fit. You are bored with your jobs and bothered that you aren't where you think you should be in life. Out of necessity, you have gravitated to whatever job you could lay your hands on. Sometimes working two jobs at the same time. (Food is important!)

You find yourself stressed out, struggling to pay the bills, wondering if this is all that life holds for you. (Don't worry. It isn't.) You know that you have more to offer the world. You are enthusiastic. You have a million and one great ideas. You have the guts to go out and get what you want, but how do you figure out what that is?

This book is for you, too.

You should know that I am not judging you. I have been in your shoes. I get it. I have been exhausted, frustrated, unfulfilled, and broke. I held multiple jobs at once and struggled to support my family. I knew, deep down, that I had the drive to be more and do more. I just didn't know where I was headed. Maybe you don't know where you are headed career-wise either. But you don't have to live your life this way. **You don't have to live a life of desperation. You can decide to change your destiny. I did.**

I am no longer a pizza delivery guy...

You won't find me ringing your doorbell at midnight with a warmed-over pie. I don't drive a forklift anymore (even though it is a pretty fun vehicle to operate). I no longer work long days, dead-tired from stirring batches of detergent in a chemical plant. In the last decade, I have become one of the top tier sellers in my industry. I now have that MBA, tucked neatly in my pocket.

I have gone from aimlessly job-hopping to launching a solid career. I have found my purpose and path. I have taken on a leadership role in my company and collaborate with million-dollar clients. Now instead of wondering where I am heading with my life, I am passionate about helping others get to where they want to go.

And for those of you who feel like you don't have enough schooling or that the schooling you have didn't prepare you for your career, don't despair. What I have learned in the last twenty years, the life-altering power skills that I want to share with you, weren't learned in a graduate program, or a college classroom, or a seminar. These skills were learned through trial and error (and more error). They were learned during sales calls, in mentoring sessions, team meetings, as I put each skill into play.

These skills have revolutionized the way that I think. They have influenced the way I interact with my clients. Their impact has spilled over into my family life and personal relationships.

I am the person I am supposed to be right now.
I am becoming the person I am meant to be.

WHO ARE YOU?

Take a deep breath right now. Imagine a different career scenario for yourself. Imagine that you are able to navigate your day with a sense of calm and purpose.

- You know who you are.
- You know where your natural gifts and talents lie.
- You are passionate about your work, even with its ups and downs.
- You are engaged with the people you work with and collaborate regularly.
- You are on a path of learning and loving it.
- You are a problem solver and critical thinker.
- You maintain upbeat work relationships and still have time for investing in your family at home.
- You share a mutually supportive relationship with your boss.
- You thrive even when change upends your day.
- You remain calm in tense situations.
- You see problems as opportunities to help make things better.

- You are motivated and positive.
- You are empathetic and caring.
- •You find joy in the day-to-day ins and outs of your job and flourish where you are.

This imagined scenario could be your future. It is not outside the realm of possibility.

YOUR DECISION DAY

You were designed for accomplishment, engineered for
success, and endowed with seeds of greatness.

— ZIG ZIGLAR

Life doesn't always end up going the way that you think it will. You don't get to decide where you are born, who your family is, what socioeconomic status you are born into, or what opportunities will come your way. But no matter what hand you have been dealt, **you get to decide who you become.** While a whole lot of folks may influence you in your decision-making process... ultimately, it is your decision to make.

My own disappointing career opportunities compelled me to a life-altering decision. A choice that catapulted my life in a different direction and set me on the path of self-discovery. It all started on a hot, humid day on a forklift in a chemical plant parking lot...

My Decision Day

At the ripe old age of twenty-one, I had two years of junior college under my belt and a smattering of work experience. The upside was that I had just met and married the girl of my dreams. My brother, who knew her from church, told me I needed to meet her because her mom made sweet tea and slaw like our mom. I could have cared less about the slaw. Michelle was the prettiest girl around. I left our first date at the county fair, thinking, "I could take her home and marry her tonight." A year later, we were married, starting our life together with big dreams and a shoe-string budget. As she finished college, we lived in a tiny apartment, and I worked two dead-end jobs that each paid about $7.50 an hour.

During the day, I worked at a small chemical plant with about eight employees. Being a small team operation, I ran a forklift, helped with shipping and receiving, packaged materials, and mixed our product. I spent long days mixing chemicals to create detergents. I followed each recipe using powder form chemicals, putting the right raw material mix into a large mixer located a story and a half above the production floor. Another production worker below would package it on the scale. We packaged 50-100 lb. bags of mixture, wearing dust masks all day to protect our lungs. In the brutal heat of the Missouri summer, I wore long sleeves and long pants to protect my skin. It was not a glamorous job...not by a long shot.

The plant had zero air-conditioning, and the temperatures would frequently soar into the 100's. It was hot, humid, and the floor was slippery from the chemical mixture. One of the materials we worked with was caustic and would burn your skin badly if mixed with water. The moisture in the humidity would activate the caustic. On slow days, we scraped the dangerous concrete floors that were slick with the material. We moved 100 lb. bags of detergent into 300-500 lb. drums. We loaded up the trucks. Then we would start all over again the next day. Even though I was getting the workout of my life (P90X had nothing on our team!), it was physically exhausting work. The camaraderie with my co-workers was the only thing that kept me going.

After I would clock out at the plant, I would head to my next job as a Domino's pizza delivery man. I delivered for a franchise that had seven locations. My car was an old jalopy that couldn't stand up to the hard workload. It broke down on a regular basis. The people at Auto Zone knew me by first name. They had looked me up in the system so many times they probably had my phone number memorized. I appreciated their support, but the endless repairs were draining my bank account. After a frantic night of pizza delivery, I would head home to crash. It was a very full, very hectic life with very little margin.

I was a hard worker. I put in my best effort at both jobs. I even got an employee award for my delivery efforts, but I quickly began to realize that this dual career path of detergent mixer and delivery man was headed nowhere. I could barely pay the rent. I wasn't mentally stimulated. I wasn't developing a new skillset or being offered the opportunity to build out my career path. I wasn't going where I wanted to go. I wasn't becoming the person I knew I could be.

I was **clowning around** with my life.
I was **clowning around** with my future and the future of my family.
I was **clowning around** with my destiny.
For anything to shift in my life, for anything to change, I was going to have to decide to
stop clowning around.

What Do You Mean by "Clowning Around?"

Let me give you some context, since more likely than not, you are thinking, *Please... don't make this book be about clowns. I don't even like clowns. They weird me out. They are so creepy with their giant shoes and murderous tendencies.* Good point.

First of all, let me say that evil clown movies with gross plots and blood-thirsty endings have given the age-old artistry of clowning a bad rap. Back in the day, clowns were all about hilarity, pratfalls, and cotton candy. *And who doesn't love side-splitting laughter with an overdose of sugar? It's a winning combo.*

I, for one, love a good clown gag and am partial to pies in the face. So, as you read this book and come across the phrase **stop clowning around**, I want you to visualize Red-Nose-Day-I-care-about-the-world-and-like-to-laugh clowning vs. Hiya-Georgie-I'm-an-alien-and-I-eat-children … clowning. *Got it?* Good.

Let me give you a little background into how "clowning around" has shaped my own life. When I was a kid, my parents added a clown act to their weekly children's ministry to bolster creativity and fun. Born in the heart of middle America, I was raised with strong family values and even stronger church ties. Service and community were the themes that our lives were built around. Everyone in our family was a part of the team.

From the age of ten on, you could find me singing, serving, and working the Sunday School crowd for laughs. I loved every minute of it. The more I messed up? The more I goofed around? The more pie that went up my nose? The better the Sunday.

When I got my hands on the Ringling Brothers Barnum and Bailey Circus' *How to Be A Clown* video, revealing the secrets of clowning from makeup to juggling, I thought I had arrived. I studied each frame, each skill, each technique. I wanted to be the best clown I could be. Red nose and all.

Clowning was so much a part of my growing up experience that the vernacular worked its way into our family life. There was a time for clowning (on the stage), and there was a time for getting serious (real life). My siblings and I couldn't seem to keep them straight. **On a regular basis, my mom would look in me in the eye (not laughing at all) and say, "Stop clowning around."** I knew what this meant.

Stop clowning around meant I needed to **STOP** doing whatever crazy, counter-productive activity I was doing...

- bugging my siblings
- procrastinating
- making a mess
- yelling and screaming
- punching people
- tearing through the house
- ignoring what my mom asked me to do

And **START** doing something productive...

- calming down
- cleaning up
- helping others
- spreading love, joy, and peace,
- finishing my homework
- and mostly, doing the dishes like I had been asked.

Mom was expecting me to be the person that she knew I could be. She was always interested in my character and the person that I was becoming. She was greatly invested in the outcome.

But I was the one who determined the outcome. My choices. My behaviors. My attitude. These factors set the course for my success.

Delivery, Detergent, or Destiny? (The question that altered the course of my life)

Fast forward ten years, and my "clowning around" attitude had worked its way into my adult life. I was pouring countless hours into a work-life that wasn't producing the results that I wanted or needed. But this time, I didn't have my mom regulating my choices or my behaviors. It was all me. *How could I make the changes I needed to make? How does someone set out to change the course of their career? And what was the moment that motivated me to make that life-altering decision?*

One summer day, I was loading a shipment into a customer's truck at the chemical plant. He was a slim, white-haired gentleman in his fifties. I had seen him around before when he would come in to pick up a shipment. Sweating in the Missouri heat, I finished loading up the detergent in his truck. He came around the side of the forklift for a chat. I love people and getting to talk with the customers was a highpoint, in an otherwise, lackluster day. At the end of our conversation, he stopped and looked right at me.

Then he asked me the question that altered the course of my life.

"What are you doing here, anyway?"

I was caught off guard and answered, "**What?**"

He said, "**You're in a blue-collar role, and you are as white-collar as they come. Why are you working here?**"

I sat there… stunned. I didn't know how to respond. *Why was I working here? What was I doing? If this random guy could see that I was working the wrong job, why couldn't I? If he knew I had the potential to be more and do more, why didn't I?*

I felt a sense of pride (the good kind), boiling up in my chest. I felt something shift in my mind and my outlook. That man's question opened up a new world for me. It was partnered with a sense of hope.

I could be more. I could do more. I just had to decide I was going to do it.

That day would change the trajectory of my life. The change didn't happen overnight. I did not take the sales world by storm by the time I was twenty-two. (Shocking, I know!) But it did bring about an elemental shift in my thought process. His words of affirmation challenged my belief in myself.

I began looking at myself and at my life in a new way. I started to seek opportunities that would challenge me. I began to educate myself. I started to read books that could help me grow. (On one trip to the flea market, I stumbled upon two books that would shape my entire career outlook… but more on those books in chapter 3!) I began to embrace the idea that I was meant for leadership. I began to learn the set of skills that would build out my career. (The super skills that I can't wait to share with you.)

All I needed to do was...

Stop clowning around and start becoming the person I was meant to be.

Your Decision Day

Today, in this moment, you are the one who is greatly invested in the outcome of your own life. And you are the one who will determine the outcome of your own life with... **Your choices. Your behaviors. Your attitude.**

Even now, you are charting the course for your future success. You know that there is more inside of you to give. You may not know what direction you want to go in, but you know that you are longing for bigger challenges and greater impact with your life and career. Maybe you don't have a white-haired gentleman asking you a life-altering question that will catapult you into your future.

So... I will.

What are you doing here, anyway?
What is it that you are dreaming of?
What inner potential remains untapped deep inside
of you?

You have the unique opportunity to change the way that you look at your life... today. Your decision will impact your work, your boss, your co-workers, your career, and your work/life balance.

You can drop the counter-productive craziness that fills your work life. You can embrace the leadership potential that lies within you. You can make the decision that will change the trajectory of your life today.

All you have to do is stop clowning around and become the master of your show.

THE STOP CLOWNING AROUND MINDSET

Get Dissatisfied
Do Something Different
Become Your Own Champion
Let Your Future Shape Your Present
Face Your Fear

GET DISSATISFIED

There is a certain amount of dissatisfaction that goes with knowing your time, talent and abilities are not being properly used.

— ZIG ZIGLAR

On yet another sweltering summer day, shortly after the encounter I had with the white-haired gentleman, my wife, Michelle, and I found ourselves wandering through stalls of the Pevely Flea Market. One of our simple pleasures as a young married couple was going to garage sales and thrifting. We would spend our Saturdays scavenging local sales and flea markets. We loved the thrill of the hunt. Getting a good deal was an adrenaline hit. Our little apartment was a testament to my wife's ingenuity and creativity when it came to converting junk to treasure. (You tend to get creative when you are living off minimum wage.)

The flea market had taken over an old drive-in movie parking lot and boasted almost an acre of buildings and tents. Hundreds of vendors showed up each weekend to sell and haggle. (*Haggling tip: Don't ever pay what is on the ticket. Bartering is expected!*) You never knew what kind of treasure you would find for under a buck. Antique oil cans, fresh fruit, vintage tablecloths, Tonka trucks, weathered tools, cleaning supplies... you name it; they had it. The smell of kettle corn lingered in the air (yet another reason to love flea market shopping), and the tantalizing thought of scoring the next deal led us from stall to stall. My wife stopped to ask a vendor a question about a piece of furniture, so I wandered into the booth next door, glancing around to take in what they were offering. I was searching for books.

Now let me take a moment to remind you, *I didn't even read books at this point in my life.*

The last thing my 21-year-old-college-dropout self would have ever wanted to do was pick up another meaningless, mind-numbing book.

If you recall, during my young adult years, I found sleeping more enjoyable than learning. In the battle of pillows vs.

books, pillows had always won. But ever since that pivotal forklift conversation, things had been shifting for me. I had been thinking more about my life, in general.

I was wrestling with what kind of future my current employment offered me. (Looming bills, overwhelming workload, minimal family time, monotonous tasks…) I was reaching a place where I was no longer comfortable with who I was becoming or where I was going.

I wanted more. I wanted to be more. I wanted to do more.

I was becoming dissatisfied.

Dissatisfied:

aggrieved, discontented, disgruntled, displeased, malcontented

---

Positive Dissatisfaction

Dissatisfaction is often seen as a negative state to be in. When you think of being dissatisfied, you may think that means being grumpy, irritated, and bummed out. No one wants that. The type of dissatisfaction I am talking about is a positive thing. The moment that you become dissatisfied with what you are doing and who you are becoming, you are in a powerful place, because in the right circumstances, **dissatisfaction is a great motivator**. If you use it correctly, it can be the launch point into your future. Ask yourself these questions:

- Are you thriving in your current work environment?
- Do you see a growth pattern in your future that offers advancement?
- Are you finding yourself challenged creatively and mentally by your job?
- Are you able to envision a positive future for yourself staying on your present career path?
- Is your character and skill level being developed and strengthened in your field?
- Are you having positive interactions with your managers and co-workers?
- Is your job a good fit for your natural talents and gifts?
- Are you thriving in the area of work/life balance?
- Do you have a passion and purpose for the work that you are doing?

If you answered "no" to any of the above, take some time to ponder why you answered that way.

- Is your answer a momentary "no" that is likely to improve?
- Or is your answer a resounding "no" that will not likely change…unless you make a change?

Now, you may answer these questions and feel like you are stuck in dead-end space with nowhere to go.

DON'T BELIEVE IT!

You may feel the pull to fall into a disabling depression at your current state of affairs.

DON'T DO IT!

Depression paralyzes you, keeping you stuck where you are. Fight those feelings of despair and let dissatisfaction take over, instead. Allow your dissatisfaction to catapult you towards change. Dissatisfaction wants to kick depression's butt.

When you are dissatisfied, you are no longer buying into the lie that you can't change and neither can your situation.

Instead:

- You are recognizing your worth.
- You are recognizing that you have more to offer this world than what you are giving right now.
- You are recognizing that you are a valuable individual with talents and skills that CAN and SHOULD be developed.

(Go ahead and kick depression's butt. It deserves it.)

If you see that you are stagnating where you are, unchallenged by your work, stuck in a lane that underutilizes your gifts, or unable to stand out in the position you are currently holding… GET DISSATISFIED!

Top 10 Markers of Job Satisfaction

In a 2019 workplace satisfaction study, Aerotek, a recruiting and staffing company that works with over 300,000 contract employees, asked 1200 workers across various careers and industries to indicate the top factors of their job satisfaction. Across the board, the top ten markers of job satisfaction came back as follows[1]:

1. Business practices in line with my values
2. Opportunities for growth and advancement
3. My ideas taken seriously
4. Recognition for my work
5. Manager(s) care about my career
6. Transparent communication about job and company
7. Compensation in line with expectations
8. Gaining marketable skills
9. Clear communication about what is expected
10. Gaining a broad spectrum of skills

(As we move ahead, we will be focusing on essentials #8 and #10… which will actually have a huge impact on essentials #1-7 & 9… but I am getting ahead of myself!)

I will be honest, if I had been a part of the study above, very few of those positive workplace factors were being met by my own environment when I was sweating my face off over a vat of caustic at twenty-one. Getting dissatisfied with who I was and where I was, wasn't all that difficult for me.

Dissatisfaction and Negativity are Two Different Things

Have you ever been around a friend who endlessly complains about their crazy boss, their lame co-workers, their jacked-up company, and how they can't stand their dead-end job... but they just keep working there? Frustrating, isn't it? As the listener, you are probably thinking things like, *I can't take one more minute of your negativity and you are bumming me out!*

By inviting you to be dissatisfied with your present situation, I am not suggesting that you become the friend that bums everyone out. I am not giving you license to be ungrateful and negative.

In order to get where you want to go, you are going to need all the gratitude and positivity you can muster. (Negativity tends to be best friends with depression... remember that dissatisfaction wants to kick depression's butt!)

- You can be grateful for all that you have and have been given, and still be dissatisfied.
- You can even be thankful for the stressed-out space you are in, because you know you are not willing to stay in that space, and you are going to do something about it.
- You can be positive that there are great possibilities in your future, and still be dissatisfied.

Dissatisfaction (not negativity) is the key to realizing that in order to fulfill your potential, you are going to have to make a shift.

Are You A Part of This Trend?

Employee satisfaction is one of the buzz words that companies are interested in right now. *Why?* Because happy, satisfied employees mean up to a 12% increase in work production![2] In 2018, the Conference Board survey of 1500 American workers showed a steady rise in job satisfaction for the 8th year in a row.[3] That's a whole lot of people who were happier and more satisfied with where they than they were in 2010. In 2010, 36% percent of the workers surveyed were satisfied with their jobs. In 2018's survey, 51% were happy at work. That is a 15% increase in job satisfaction over the last decade.

If we do the math, (it's not geometry, so I can handle it), that is 225 people who weren't satisfied with where they were at eight years ago, and now they are. That is an upward trend in job satisfaction.

The question is... are you a part of this trend? Would you place yourself in the satisfied 51% of that survey? If not, I invite you to embrace a little healthy dissatisfaction. (It worked for me!)

The moment you realize that you are not becoming the person you are meant to be is the moment that you can decide to change your life.

Why I Was Dissatisfied

I had always been a hard worker. I would put 110% into whatever job was in front of me. But 110% of being a pizza delivery man and detergent mixer wasn't enough anymore. I was dissatisfied because:

- I wanted to provide for my family beyond a survival level
- I wanted more time with my wife
- I wanted to be mentally stimulated by my work
- I wanted more opportunity for growth and advancement
- I wanted to find a passion and purpose for what I was doing

As I combed the stalls of that crowded flea market, I had reached a turning point.

I was willing to change...

My choices. My behaviors. My attitude.

I knew that the person I was, wasn't the person I wanted to be anymore. I knew if I wanted my employment opportunities, my work/life balance, my circumstances to change? **It was up to me.**

And if you want your employment opportunities, your work/life balance, and your circumstances to change? It is up to you.

It is never too late to be who you might have been.

— GEORGE ELLIOT

The question to ask yourself as you head into the next chapter is this:

Are you willing to change?

Your choices, your behaviors, and your attitude are not only shaping your present, they are determining your future. If you are dissatisfied with where you are and who you are at present, you have the opportunity to launch yourself into a different future.

But if you are dissatisfied and unwilling to change?

- You will stay the same person that you are.
- You will continue to be in the same place.
- You will continue to do the same things.
- And you will get the same results. (Super frustrating, right?!!)

If you are at the point in your life, where you are ready for your story to shift, to take responsibility for your own life, then by all means, turn the page. Because once you are willing to change? All bets are off in your quest for growth, leadership, and standing out in your field.

Stop clowning around and get dissatisfied!

DO SOMETHING DIFFERENT

If you want to be different, do something different.

— WYNTON MARSALIS

S o, you are ready to make a change. That is fantastic, because one of the most universally known anonymous quotes is the definition of insanity.

Insanity =
doing the same thing over and over again and expecting different results.

If you want something in your life (job, personal development, family life, relationships) to change? **You have to take responsibility for your life.** Your friends and family, your boss, and co-workers don't have a say in who you are choosing to become at this point. It is all up to you.

If you think that you can keep embracing the same behaviors and making the same choices, and get different results each time? You may be a little crazy. (I'm just saying).

Are You Scared of Change?

In the *Harvard Business Review* article, "10 Reasons People Resist Change," author and Harvard professor, Rosabeth Moss Kantor, shares the most common reasons people run from doing something different.[1]

People are afraid of:

1. A loss of control.
2. Uncertainty in their circumstances.
3. Sudden changes and their inability to prepare for the consequences.
4. Change upsetting their routines and habits.
5. A loss of face or dignity.
6. Being incompetent in a new setting.
7. More work.
8. How changing their lives will affect others.
9. That past resentments will be revealed in the process.
10. Being hurt or of losing something that they already have.

Fear can be the thing that holds you back from becoming all that you are meant to be. Don't let it!

Be more afraid of NOT becoming who you are meant to be, than of doing something different.

Let your fear of staying the same person, in the same place, with the same results, set the course for a new future.

Action is a great restorer and builder of confidence.

Inaction is not only the result, but the cause, of fear.

Perhaps the action you take will be successful;

perhaps different action or adjustments will have to follow.

But any action is better than no action at all.

— NORMAN VINCENT PEALE

Doing Something Different

When I entered the flea market stall on our Saturday flea market trip, I did something different. Glancing at the books on the table in front of me, two caught my eye. *Think and Grow Rich* by Napoleon Hill and *How I Raised Myself from Failure to Success in Selling by Frank* Bettger. (I don't know about you, but the possibilities of being successful and using my mind to grow rich were intriguing.)

Both books were ten cents each, a steal, as far as I was concerned. Looking back now, I know that Hill's and Bettger's books were the concrete representation of their "doing something different." In that moment, I followed their lead. I did something different. **I bought both books.**

Napoleon Hill's Story

Think and Grow Rich is a compilation of wisdom from the most successful achievers of the early 1900's, collected by Napoleon Hill. He became one of the greatest self-help writers of the 20th century, but not without overcoming his own struggles and hardships. Born in 1883, Napoleon's mom died when he was ten years old. He was left without a champion and a compass. His early teenage years found him floundering and rebelling. His father didn't know how to take care of him or encourage him. It was his stepmom who stepped in pushed him to get a writing job. He became a fledgling reporter by the age of fifteen.[2]

Hill claims that interviewing Andrew Carnegie in 1908, the steel magnate and billionaire, changed the course of his life. (Decision day for Napoleon Hill!) Carnegie's rags to riches journey as a Scottish immigrant to a business tycoon and philanthropist was riveting. Hill was inspired by all that Carnegie accomplished. He was still struggling himself, as a law school dropout and aspiring writer. His journey had been marked by financial difficulties and disappointment. **He needed to do something different.**

Legend has it that Carnegie challenged him to interview the greatest successes of the century and discover the philosophy of achievement that linked them all together. Napoleon spent the next twenty years doing just that.

Hill interviewed Thomas Edison, Alexander Graham Bell, George Eastman, Henry Ford, Elmer Gates, John D. Rockefeller, Charles M. Schwab, F.W. Woolworth, Theodore Roosevelt, and Woodrow Wilson. The resulting book was *Think and Grow Rich.* The one which I held in my hand.

Around the same time that Napoleon Hill was interviewing Andrew Carnegie, Frank Bettger's story was just getting started...

Frank Bettger's Story

Frank Bettger was a baseball player who was fired in 1907 after a short, ineffective season, playing for the Tri-State minor league. He was completely caught off guard by his termination. A good player who tried his best, Bettger couldn't figure out why he had been fired. He went to talk to his manager. His manager told him he was fired because he was lazy and moved like a washed-up twenty-year vet of the game.

Frank was flabbergasted. He told his manager, he wasn't lazy! He was so nervous and scared. He was paralyzed. He was trying to hide his fear from the crowd and his teammates by acting nonchalant and taking it easy. His manager told him that wasn't working for him. He said, "Whatever you do after you leave here, for heaven's sake, wake yourself up and put some life and enthusiasm into your work!" **Frank needed to do something different!**

Frank's next baseball gig was with the Atlantic League. His league demotion meant a pay cut from $175 a month to $25 a month. His first time on the field, he remembered his manager's words. Even though he was scared, he didn't let that hold him back. He was determined to be a different player. No one would ever call him lazy again.

Frank said, "From the moment I appeared on the field, I acted like a man electrified. I acted as though I were alive with a million batteries. I threw the ball around the diamond so fast and so hard that it almost knocked our infielders' hands apart." His enthusiasm lit up the whole team. The team went on to a victory.

In the local newspaper article that came out the next day, **Atlantic League's new enthusiastic player was given the nickname "Pep" Bettger.** Frank cut out the article and sent it to his old manager. With his new energetic style of play, his pay was raised to $185 a month. Within two years, he was drafted to Major Leagues and played with even greater enthusiasm for the St. Louis Cardinals.

Four years later, after being transferred to the Chicago Cubs, he experienced a career-ending injury to his arm. *While he was devasted at the time, Frank said later that is was one of the greatest events of his life.*[3]

Frank began a new career selling life insurance. It was rough going. Selling was a tough racket. **Again, he was at a place in his life where he realized he needed to do something different.**

Frank remembered what his old baseball manager told him about putting life and energy into his work. He began applying the lessons he had learned in baseball, admitting his fear, using enthusiasm, and endless practicing, to advance his sales career.

With practice, with his trademark pep, and with an eye for applying life lessons to his selling career, Frank became a top seller in his field. He began touring and giving sales talks with Dale Carnegie, the renowned motivational speaker and author of the bestseller *How to Win Friends and Influence People.* He went on to write bestsellers himself. His first book shared the lessons he learned in baseball and how they shaped his selling career. It was called *How I Raised Myself from Failure to Success in Selling.* My second purchase at the flea market.

My Story

That twenty-cent purchase began my journey of doing things differently. I took those books home. Then I did something different... again. *I read them both cover to cover.* It is funny how other people's stories can inspire you to re-write your own. I don't think my wife knew what was going on. I'm not sure I did, either. I just knew that doing something different was the only way that my life was going to change. I was in the embryonic moments of my career. That twenty-cent investment would yield immeasurable benefits in the future.

After pouring over the books, I started thinking differently about myself... my job... my goals. *Think and Grow Rich* author Napoleon Hill says that **a goal is a dream with a deadline.** My thinking was shifting from survival mode to goal-oriented. My thoughts changed from, "How can I get through today?" to "How can I have a better tomorrow?" and "What do I need to do to get there?"

Your Story

You may be wondering where your nearest flea market is at this point. Maybe you can pick up some cheap-o books that will radically change the course of your life. My hope is that this book will do that for you! But you don't need to go to a flea market to start doing something different.

Doing something different is simply changing your behavior in a positive direction... one that could open doors to a new way of thinking about yourself and your life.

Whatever you did yesterday and the day before... and the day before...and the day before... that didn't yield the results you were looking for?

Skip it. Stop the insanity!

Do something different today so that your tomorrow can have a different outcome.

Stop clowning around and do something different!

BECOME YOUR OWN CHAMPION

Champion comes from the Latin word *campionem* for "gladiator, fighter."

C hampion – Noun or Verb?

The English word, *champion, stems from the Latin root campio*, meaning gladiator or fighter.[1] In the case of the gladiator in the coliseum? It meant a fight to the death. (Think Russell Crowe in *Gladiator*. It was pretty grisly.) Down through the centuries, the word *champion* became more of a winner-takes-all noun, (Think *Rocky*. Yo, Adrian!). The best of the best. Fight to the finish. Undefeated (Think *Rocky II, III, IV & V!*) Being a champion (the noun version)), means going all out, no matter what the challenge, no matter who the opponent, and being victorious.

In the last 200 hundred years, *champion,* the noun, evolved into *champion,* the verb. Now, it is not just something you are, it is something you do. When you champion a cause, (Think *Erin Brockovich*), you are fighting, protecting, defending, maintaining, or supporting that belief, or ideal. When you champion a person? You are fighting on behalf of someone – their best interests, their hopes, their dreams, and their rights.

What Does Championing A Cause Have to Do with You?

Sometimes when you try to do something different, to make a shift, to change up your life, it feels less like an adventure in self-development and more like an out and out brawl – sometimes with yourself...sometimes with the people around you.

For those of you who like to avoid conflict, both inner conflict and conflict with others, just remember that fighting for something you believe in actually a good thing. As you enter this new phase of doing something different, remind yourself that you are going to, more than likely, be in for a fight, and that just proves that...

YOU ARE CHANGING.

Expect it and accept it. Change rarely comes easy. You will have to fight your fear, fight your apathy, fight your uncertainty, and fight your own old habits. Like a gladiator facing an opponent in the coliseum, it is not so much a fight to the death, as it is a fight for your life. The life that you want to have. A fight for your goals. Your dreams. Your future.

You are going to need to be your own champion.

What a Champion Looks Like

Ray Goforth, Mensa member and advocate, says, "**There are two types of people who will tell you that you cannot make a difference in this world: those who are afraid to try and those who are afraid you will succeed.**"

When Ray was a twelve-year-old boy, he found himself stranded on a road trip to Oregon with his mother and sister. Their car had broken down and they barely managed to make it to a repair shop. Ray's mom, a single mom, had enough money for the part, but not for the repairs. She asked the shop owner if she could buy the part and make the repair herself. He said no. He closed up shop and Ray's family prepared to spend the night in their car.[2]

To their amazement, one of the shop's mechanics returned with his own tools and helped them get their car started. That mechanic went out of his way to help Ray's family, bucking what his boss said, and finding another way to bring hope to their dire situation. That moment impacted Ray for the rest of his life. He determined to be the type of person who went out of his way to help others.

While Ray's life had been comfortable before his parents divorced, that shifted when his mom became a single parent. There were years of struggle and hardship that he faced. Ray was turned away from a private hospital in his teenage years, because he couldn't afford his asthma treatment. With little parental direction, he also struggled to find his path, waiting five years after high school to attend college.

But Ray's drive wasn't waylaid. He wanted a different future for himself. He became his own champion. He graduated with a law degree. His wife, that he met in college, joined him in his pursuit of justice. That value of helping others that was impressed on him at an early age, played into his career path. He is now the Executive Director of the SPEAA, a labor union, that advocates for over 26,000 aerospace professionals. He is not only fighting for his own future, but for the future of others.

He didn't let his circumstances or the lack of belief others had in him hold him back. Ray became his own champion.

Becoming My Own Champion

My fight for my future began when I approached my boss at the chemical plant. Energized and emboldened by the books I had been reading, I wanted to take my future into my own hands. I was nervous, but I was ready.

Coming off a long shift on the plant floor, I stood in front of my boss and told him I was interested in a new line of work. I looked him in the eye and asked, "Are there any sales positions available in the company?" I had a sense that because I liked helping people, that I might be good in sales.

He laughed and said, "You wouldn't be a good fit for sales."

I felt the heat rise in my face. He wasn't trying to be a jerk.

He just didn't know me.

He didn't know what my future would hold.

He didn't know what I was capable of.

His laughter ended our conversation, but those words lit the fire that still burns in me to this day. **That was the day I became my own champion.**

I left the company a few months later, knowing that I would show him. I knew there was more to me than he saw, than he ever thought I could be. I would love to run into him now and let him know I'm not only one of the sales leaders within my company, but my entire industry. I think he would be shocked. But that is what happens when you become your own champion. Your future looks amazingly different from your past.

Why Should You Advocate for Yourself?

Govloop.com, an online network that serves over 300,000 government leaders, promoting problem-solving, collaboration, and career advancement, says that there are benefits for sticking up for yourself.[3]

1. **It may benefit your career in the long run.** That raise you are looking for? The promotion you deserve? It could hinge on you speaking up. You will never know what you can acquire or achieve until you are brave enough to ask for it.
2. **You will gain a life-long skill.** Confrontation, used healthily, not only benefits you in the workplace but in life. There will always be situations when you need to stand up for yourself and not just regarding your career. Practicing advocacy builds confidence in those situations.
3. **People need to know if they are acting unfairly.** If a colleague is treating you poorly or if your compensation package doesn't meet industry standards, you should be able to stand up for yourself. This isn't being pushy or over-sensitive, advocating for yourself in these kinds of situations helps those around you recognize that you value yourself.

Dare to Become Your Own Champion

You may never have your boss laugh in your face when you ask for a promotion or a pay raise, but you can still become your own champion. **Your fight for your future begins the**

moment you stop clowning around and start fighting for the person you are meant to become.

One of the most important things that you can learn to do while reading this book (and in life!) is to realize that *no one can stop you from taking ownership of your own life and path.* No one can decide your journey for you. No one else can write your story for you.

You can seek advice and help from others, but real change starts to occur in you when you become your own champion. You are fighting for the life you are destined for. You are fighting to become the you that you were meant to be.

This is important because your colleagues, your boss, and co-workers may not have the same vision for your life that you do. They may not say the words, "I don't think you will succeed," to your face, but their actions tell you otherwise. They may warn you that change is hard, that it is better to be content with the job you have, or subtly discourage you from trying new things.

This may be because they can't imagine you in a different light or simply because when you change your life, it will disrupt their own.

Those who are the most well-meaning, your friends and family members, may discourage you from doing something different because they want to protect you. They don't want to see you get hurt or be disappointed.

Their dreams for you may be different from your own. They may see change as being too risky.

I would say that at this point in your life...**you can't risk NOT changing.**

Your future depends on it.

You will need to fight for who you want to become and all that you can achieve. You will need to advocate for yourself and search out opportunities to grow and challenge yourself. Start advocating for yourself right now. In this moment.

Stop clowning around and become your own champion!

LET YOUR DREAM OF THE FUTURE SHAPE YOUR PRESENT

All successful people, men and women, are big dreamers. They imagine what their future could be, ideal in every respect, and then they work every day toward their distant vision, that goal, or purpose.

— BRIAN TRACY

Big Picture, Small Steps

Here you are, at this moment, dissatisfied in a good way, ready for change, prepared to take that next big step and...now what? You know what you don't want

your life to look like, but you are *not sure what life you want.*
This is the fun part!

This is the moment where you **start dreaming big, bold dreams and start facing your fear.** (We'll talk about facing fear in Chapter 6!)

Let the vision of your future shape your life's trajectory.

Think **big picture** (what do I want my life to look and feel like in the next five, ten, twenty years?) and **start taking small steps** (dreaming and facing your fear) towards making that big picture your future.

Thinking about the future can lend itself to great fear and trepidation. The future is the vast unknown. It can seem full of uncertainty. It can feel daunting. Maybe you are the type of person who likes the security of knowing what is coming next. You feel like dreaming is unrealistic, since you are unsure of what you can accomplish. Or you would rather not dream at all, since you might get your hopes up and be disappointed.

I will say this as we start this chapter. If you *decide NOT to dream?*

You will absolutely be disappointed by your future.

Let's just get that out of the way up front. Life does not come to any of us without uncertainty, change, challenges, and some drama. (This is real life we are talking about.) You don't have a choice about what has happened in your past. But you have a choice about who and what you will be in your future.

What you do, say, and think about your today will shape your tomorrow.

So why wouldn't you decide to

Dream big, bold dreams about your future,
knowing that it will impact your life for the better?

You may be thinking,

- What if the future doesn't turn out how I want it to?
- What if I try new things and fail?
- What if I don't accomplish all I set out to do?
- What if I can't lead like I think can?
- What if I can't meet up to my own expectations?

What if? What if? What if?

Let's take a minute and get out of that fight or flight mindset that fear induces. Take a deep breath. Exhale. And now let's switch up those "what if" questions. Ask yourself these questions instead:

- What if the future turns out better than I can possibly imagine?
- What if I let failure be a starting point instead of a stopping point?
- What if I try new things and discover my passion?

- What if I accomplish all I set out to do and then some?
- What if I am able to tap into my own leadership ability in a way that impacts my life and the lives of those around me in a positive way?
- What if I surpass my own expectations?

WHAT IF? WHAT IF? WHAT IF?

When you think of your future, remember that you are taking charge of your life, your career, and your destiny. You get to decide what kind of "what if" questions shape your future.

Now ask yourself this question:

What if I start dreaming big, bold dreams for my future...today?

First, think. Second, dream. Third, believe. And finally, dare.

— WALT DISNEY

Start Dreaming Big Bold Dreams

One of the greatest dreamers of this past century was Walt Disney. *How does a kid from the suburbs of Chicago go from selling pictures door-to-door to his neighbors to selling movies to the world? How does a newspaper cartoonist make the leap to animation studio owner? How does a movie studio mogul build an amusement park empire?*

He starts dreaming. The crazy thing about fulfilled dreams? They open the doors to new bigger, bolder dreams. Walt said, **"If you can visualize it, if you can dream it, then there's some way to do it."**[1]

Walt Disney's childhood dreams of being an artist launched a 130-billion-dollar corporation that has spanned the past century and still shapes our media and culture today. (Not bad for a high school dropout!) He built out his life by dreaming big, bold dreams. He dreamt things that had never been dreamt before. Then he put in the work that made those dreams come true. When asked about his methods of making his dreams a reality, Walt said, **"People often ask me if I know the secret of success and if I could tell others how to make their dreams come true. My answer is you do it by working."**[2]

The making of Walt's dream come true didn't involve magic or pixie dust. He put feet to his dreams and marched towards a better future, dreaming big and working hard. It wasn't that his dreams went unchallenged. It wasn't that he wasn't afraid. It wasn't that he didn't fail. He just kept dreaming anyway.

Disney's career started on the heels of WWI, where he had experienced the chaos of war as a teenager, driving an ambulance for the Red Cross. In his twenties, he overcame the bankruptcy of his first animation company. With the dissolution of his company, Disney uprooted himself and his team from Missouri and moved across the country to Hollywood. His new studios weathered the Great Depression, the impact of WW2, and the 1941 strike of his animators that impacted the company for years.[3] And the dreams kept coming. He kept looking to the future, pushing forward, dreaming bigger... dreaming bolder.

Walt kept dreaming until the end of his life. When Walt Disney passed away in 1966, his dream of Disney World's Epcot Center was mid-production. The doors opened in 1971. His dreams outlived his lifetime. The impact of his bold, beautiful dreams is still felt around the world today.

Dreams are powerful things. **When you start dreaming, you have no idea what impact you will have on your future or on those around you.**

Maybe your dreams aren't Disney big. You may not think of yourself as a dreamer all. **Reframe how you think about dreaming.** Dreaming doesn't have to be all rainbows and unicorns. When it comes to dreaming about your future, it can look a whole lot like thinking (very logically) about the possibilities that your life holds.

Prospection: The act of anticipating, the act of viewing, the act of exploring (as for gold)

Humans have the amazing ability to think proactively about the future. *This is called* **prospection.** Thinking about the future actually produces amazing results and causes positive shifts in behavior.

Imagine anticipating your own life, looking toward the future with purpose, with goals, and with hope. This is not fantasizing or living in a state of unreality. Prospection is thinking about what you can and will accomplish when you dream big and work hard.

According to Summer Allen, Ph.D., writing and research fellow at the Greater Good Science Institute, studies show that prospection done right can lead to "making more prudent decisions, motivation and goal achievement, providing improved mental well-being, and being more generous."[4] Prospection puts you in a positive mindset about your future.

She says that when dreaming about the future with the present in mind, it shapes your choices.

- You are more likely to embrace delayed gratification.
- You are walking out your dreams for tomorrow by setting goals today.
- You are looking forward with positivity, not stuck in your past, or held back by your present.
- You are looking at life with a lens of gratefulness and generosity because that is the type of person you want to be in the future.

You are a prospector when it comes to your life and destiny, mining the ore of future possibilities.

What are your prospects?

I don't know.

How big and bold are your dreams?

You set your own boundaries. You decide your own limitations. The true power of prospection comes into being when you start putting feet to your dreams and doing the work.

The future belongs to those who believe in the beauty of their dreams.

— ELEANOR ROOSEVELT

My Big Bold Dream

When I left the chemical plant at the age of twenty-two, my dream didn't include a specific job or career path. I just knew... I wanted more.

My big dream was this:

1. I wanted more time with my family.
2. I wanted to do more challenging and meaningful work.

3. I wanted more opportunities to grow in the company I was in.
4. I wanted to thrive financially, not just survive.

I didn't have a lot of experience, but I was dreaming of being more than a forklift driver. That dream was enough to get me into gear.

I was willing to put in the work to change my own life.

I got on the phone and started making calls. I caught a break when the owner of a small manufacturing company took my call. I had a friend who knew him, and that was enough to pique his interest in me. I used what skills I had to connect with the owner (more on that in Chapter 7!), and he took a chance on me. He swung open the door to a new career path for me. I started working in sales. This job didn't pay any more than the chemical plant, but it started me on my white-collar journey and introduced me to the industry I am in today.

At the same time that I started my new job, I traded in my pizza delivery gig for night classes at my local junior college.

I knew that my dreams were bigger than my skill set and my knowledge base.

It wasn't easy or convenient, but my wife and I got into a rhythm with my schooling. (My dreams were impacting those around me!) We were willing to sacrifice our nights together for a better, bigger future. (Prospection – delayed gratification!)

My dreams of the future were shaping my decisions in the present.

Light Bulb Moment

During my first semester of junior college, I ended up in a business management class. This was the first class in my entire life that lit me up, engaging me in every way. As the professor began to lay out the principles of management, it resonated with me. I couldn't wait to hear what he had to say and implement his teachings in my work life. While I wasn't ready, mentally, or emotionally, to manage others, in those pivotal teaching moments, my dream was clarified. I knew, sitting in that stuffy junior college classroom, that **I was destined to work in business and leadership.**

That class flipped the switch for me and set the course for the rest of my studies. At the age of thirty-one, I graduated with a B.A. in Organizational Communication. I chose organizational communication over business, leaning into the hunch that all great leaders are great communicators.

My dreams were still growing, but I knew the place that I wanted to end up...communicating strategies, helping and influencing others, and leading a team – all of which needed that core skill of communication (Essential #5!).

After eight years of night school, classes had become a habit for both me and Michelle. Even though our first child had been born, we decided it would be silly for me to quit school while I had the momentum going.

Fulfilled dreams birth bigger, bolder dreams.

I spent the next four years getting my MBA from Webster University in St. Louis, Missouri.

As I was building out my management skills in the classroom, I was moving forward in the security industry. After changing companies, I landed a sales job with one of the fastest-growing security companies in the country. I got the job before I finished my course work for my bachelor's degree. The company hired me anyway because I was able to show that I was tenacious about growing and learning (Essential #3).

Along with taking steps towards completion with my night courses, I brought a vast knowledge of the industry to the table. (My dreams were influencing how my managers perceived me.) My dedication and sacrifice were opening doors to me that had been closed before. (My dreams were shaping my present.) I was on my way.

It wasn't that my dreams went unchallenged. It wasn't that I wasn't afraid. It wasn't that I didn't fail. **I just kept dreaming anyway.**

. . .

Your Big Bold Dream

Just a heads up, your big, bold dream will look absolutely nothing like Walt Disney's dream. Or my dream. Or your co-worker's dream, for that matter. Maybe your dream for the moment is simply... more. More than what you are and where you are.

That is an excellent place to start. You have no limitations or boundaries on your dreams. You are free to mine your future for a myriad of possibilities.

Use the Chapter 3 questions as a springboard to dream some new dreams. Using the list of prompts below, feel free to jot down your thoughts on:

- What does your dream work environment look like?
- What is your dream for growing and advancing in your career?
- What is your dream for being challenged creatively and mentally?
- Does staying on your present career path fit in with your dream for the future? If not, what would that career path be?
- What is your dream for your personal character and skill level being developed and strengthened in your field?
- What does your dream relationship with your managers and co-workers look like?
- What is your dream for incorporating your natural talents and gifts into your work?

- What is your dream for thriving in the area of work/life balance?
- What does your dream of working with passion and purpose look like?

Begin pondering and thinking about these new dreams. This prospection, the mining of future possibilities, those dreams you are dreaming...

WILL CHANGE YOUR PRESENT AND INFLUENCE YOUR FUTURE...

if you let them.

As you reflect on these new dreams, do these three things:

1. Use the power of your dreams to shape the choices you are making today.
2. Use the power of your dreams to motivate your actions.
3. Use the power of your dreams to move you forward and propel you into a bigger, bolder future.

And Whatever You Do... Don't Stop Dreaming!

Even if your dreams are challenged. Even if you are afraid. Even if you fail. Just keep dreaming.

All our dreams can come true if we have the courage to pursue them.

— WALT DISNEY

Stop clowning around and let your dream of the future shape your present!

FACE YOUR FEAR

You gain strength, courage and confidence by every experience in which you really stop to look fear in the face … you must do the thing you think you cannot do.

— ELEANOR ROOSEVELT

Facing Your Biggest Fears … Living Out Your Best Future

In June of 2019, 7.2 million people tuned in to watch the Flying Wallendas' brother and sister duo, Nik and Lijana Wallenda, cross a 1,300-foot-high wire, twenty-five stories above the ground in New York's Time Square. As if that wasn't enough, the high wire, tethered between two buildings, was set at an eight-story incline. Nik and

Lijana started on opposite sides of the wire and met in the middle, seventeen heart-pounding minutes into their treacherous walk. Thousands of spectators waited below with bated breath. Lijana sat down on the wire, balanced and steady so that Nik could step over her. In a tense moment, Lijana had to adjust her balancing pole that she had connected to incorrectly. Nik also adjusted his balancing pole that was slipping to one side. Once he passed, Lijana stood up, and they continued on to their respective sides.[1]

The tension in the air was palpable. Seventh generation aerial artists, they were not new to the danger of skywalking. Several family members over the last century had lost their lives in their feats of daring. (The Flying Wallendas are fearless!) Lijana in fact was performing for the first time since 2017, after a practice session for an attempt at a Guinness Book of World Records went horribly wrong.

While forming an eight-man pyramid on the high wire, a member of the team faltered and five other members of the troupe fell thirty feet, without a net. While Nik was able to catch the wire and hang on, Lijana broke every bone in her face, sustained internal bleeding, and broke her arm and leg. She wasn't expected to survive. But she did. Her stamina and will are a testament to the human spirit.

Back in this crucial moment, high above the flashing lights of Time Square, Lijana was staring down her greatest fear and setting out to accomplish a great dream in the same moment. She wanted to bring closure to the tragedy that had grounded her for over two years. She wanted to continue to perform and embrace the work that she loved.

Required to wear a safety harness by the city, her nerves were still shaky. Interviewed beforehand, Nik admitted, he wasn't sure how Lijana was going to take that first step. She admitted that stepping out onto that wire would be incredibly emotional. But in spite of her fear, Lijana was heard saying over her headset, "I've got this."[2]

The crazy thing? She did have it.

She faced her fear, accomplished the unimaginable, and walked out the future that she had imagined for herself. Amazing!

Go confidently in the direction of your dreams. Live the life you've imagined!

— HENRY DAVID THOREAU

Fantasized Experiences Appearing Real

Jack Canfield shares some revolutionary insights about fear in his book, *The Success Principles: How to Get from Where You Are to Where You Want to Be*. He says, "Fear is a very real emotion experienced by every human on earth. However, most of the fears we deal with are actually created by the imagination of our own mind. Often they are not logical or worthy of the anxiety, but we tend to create the future negative outcomes that could take place if we do or do not perform certain actions. I learned that many psychologists agree that fear stands for:

- Fantasized
- Experiences
- Appearing
- Real

The bad news is that we create our own fear, but we also are in power to put a stop to our fears and move forward."[3]

Canfield's brilliant acronym hits at the truth. So much of what we fear takes place in our imagination only. It's time to make a shift and face our fear.

Facing Your Fear

In this moment, you are staring across the precipice of change, looking towards your future. You are tired of being where you are. You are ready for a different moment or opportunity in life. The thing is sometimes that moment, or opportunity seems unattainable. You might as well be asked to walk a high wire twenty-five stories up. Things you desire, whether it is more work/life balance, a career shift, or the guts to stand up in front of your team and present without dropping into the fetal position? They seem like impossibilities. Fantasies. You are filled with doubt and trepidation.

Like Lijana Wallenda, you have goals you want to accomplish ... but you are afraid to fall ... or to fail.

(More than likely, your unmet goals will not send you plunging to your death. You can take comfort in that.)

Atychiphobia:

the abnormal, unwarranted, and persistent fear of failure.

Mindtools, a website dedicated to teaching the essential skills necessary for career excellence, says that fear of failure can show up in different ways.[4] It can present as:

- reluctance to try new things (comfort zone 101)
- self-sabotage (procrastination, anyone?)
- low self-confidence (the endless chatter in your mind that tells you there is no possible way you will achieve your goals)
- perfectionism (the unwillingness to attempt something you are not good at or able to perfect)

Do any of these behaviors sound familiar? Each of these mindsets only serves to keep you from achieving the goals and furthering the future that you have determined for yourself. (Remember how you kicked depression's butt? Go ahead and give fear the backhand it deserves.)

When you let fear chart your course? You don't go very far. You stay in a safe place. (maybe) You are in control. (not really... life shifts constantly, remember?) You often remain unchallenged and unfulfilled.

Let's be honest. **Failure stinks.** Let's be more honest.

You choosing to neglect the chance of a better future, not growing in your work, and giving up before you even try?

That stinks even worse.

No one likes to fail. That is a given. But you also can't succeed without risking failure. The two go hand-in-hand.

So, let's get real about fear. Everyone on the planet deals with it. Acknowledge that you are freaked out. And then decide that you will be okay, even if you fail, even if you don't know the outcome, even if you are scared out of your mind.

Your fear doesn't define you or make decisions for you or get to chart the course for your future. **You do.**

Fear Shmear

Most fears are caused by a perceived lack of control in any given situation. If you could determine a positive outcome for every single area of your life...you wouldn't be scared. So, let's take stock. What are you in control of right now?

Your job security? No.

Your manager? No.

Your company? Not even close.

Your family? Not really. (Ever tried to wrangle a three-year-old with anger issues? Who is in control? *See my point?*)

The economy?

The country?

The world?

The universe?

Nope. Nope. Nope. And definitely, nope.

So much affects you, and you control so little of it. No wonder you are a bit on the fearful side. (It's enough to put anyone on edge.)

You have very little control over most of the components in your life. This is true.

But what do you have control of?

YOU.
**Your mindset. Your choices. Your goals. Your behaviors.
Your job skills.**

Now is not the time to let your fears conquer you. You have everything in this moment that you need to make a shift. I am not saying that you won't be scared. Every single human gets scared. What I am saying is that you can accomplish what you want to…**IN SPITE OF YOUR FEAR.**

. . .

How Did Lijana Conquer Her Fear?

Lijana Wallenda did not show up in Times Square and attempt this stunt of magnificent proportions after two years of frolic and play. She showed up after two years of healing, rehab, and then, before the skywalk in New York City - she completed weeks of intense practice with her brother in Florida. Twice a day, they would practice the exact feat that they would attempt in Times Square.[5]

Lijana showed up to Times Square ready. She showed up prepared. Her body was healed. Her mind was focused. She had decades of practice under her belt. And even though the memory of her fall (failure) accompanied her up to the wire, she had the skill set that she needed to complete the incredible feat that she wanted to accomplish.

Her mind, body, and will were working as one to accomplish the goal that she had challenged herself with. And despite her well-founded fears, she achieved it.

It would be crazy for anyone who hadn't spent years on a high wire to try and walk across Times Square, with or without a safety harness. It wouldn't even be attemptable. You have to have a certain set of skills to walk across a high wire. You have to practice those skills daily. You have to continually prepare your mind, body, and will, to take on the challenge at hand. The same is true of the goal, the shift, the dream, the new life that you are trying to achieve.

Get Ready

You should know up front that if fear isn't determining your future, shutting down your progress, then all bets are off. *Why?* **Because you can always learn new skills.** You can always learn more, achieve more, and become more.

Learning a new skill (or honing a barely used one) IS POSSIBLE. All it takes is a goal, determination, and practice. Good old-fashioned hard work. (Remember, that thing that Walt Disney talked about when he told others how to accomplish their dreams?)

How can you face down your own fear of whatever is holding you back in this moment? **By building out the skills that will help you achieve what you want to achieve.** Your mind, body, and will can work as one to accomplish the goal that you have challenged yourself with. So…

Stop clowning around and face your fear!

CROSSING THE GAP

The wise man bridges the gap by laying out the path by means of which he can get from where he is to where he wants to go.

— J.P. MORGAN

Lijana the Conqueror

Lijana Wallenda had one goal in mind when she stepped out on the ¾ inch steel cable that night in June 2019. She wasn't going to let her fear define her. She wasn't going to let the tragedy of two years before, decide what her future would look like. The morning after her triumph of crossing the wire, she was asked about that powerful moment she spent facing her fear. She said,

"I feel like I conquered it. It didn't consume me. I could have taken that fear from falling and never walked the wire again. I could have walked away. But I wouldn't let that fear conquer me. So, I pushed through."[1]

Lijana admitted to nerves and butterflies as she waited to step out. With the voice of her brother and father encouraging her in her headset, she took a solid first step. She was scared... but she stepped out anyway. Because she knew what she was capable of.

"I remember all the training and how hard I worked, and you have to fall back on that. I knew my ability. I knew I could do it. I was well-trained."

Training, ability, and hard work grounded her in that moment of facing her fear. It can do the same for you.

<u>(Your Name Here)</u> the Conqueror

After reading the last six chapters, you have slowly but surely been ramping up for the first step in beginning your journey of crossing the gap of who you are and moving towards the person you are meant to become.

You have the stop clowning around mindset
You are ready to take your destiny into your own hands.

You now have yourself in an amazing (possibly terrifying but still amazing) place.

1. You are dissatisfied (in a good way) with where you are.
2. You are ready to do something different.
3. You are becoming your own champion.
4. You letting the dream of your future determine your present.
5. You are ready to give fear the backhand it deserves.

Gap:

separation in space, an incomplete or deficient area, a wide difference in character or attitude, a problem caused by some disparity.

Now is the time to cross the gap. The gap between your present and the goals that you laid out for yourself in Chapter 5. The gap between who you are now and the person you believe that you can become.

Lijana is living proof that anyone can step out of their comfort zone and overcome anything. Any challenges they might face.

— NIK WALLENDA

You may be thinking right now, *that sounds great...but how do I do that?*

Like Lijana Wallenda, you are ready to bring your body, mind, and will into focus. Now you can begin to build out the skills to make this all happen.

What skills, you ask? BEST. QUESTION. EVER.

Hard Skills vs. Soft Skills?

What skills do you need to cross the gap between your present and your future? There are two different skill sets required as you set out to accomplish your goals in life: hard skills and soft skills.

According to Investopedia, a key investment and financial success company, **"Soft skills are character traits and interpersonal skills** that characterize a person's relationships with other people. In the workplace, soft skills are considered to be a complement to **hard skills, which refer to a person's knowledge and occupational skills."**[2]

Let's look at the example of Lijana Wallenda. Clearly, for Lijana, there was a set of essential skills, both hard and soft, that she had to have to be able to walk on a high wire.

She needed a keen sense of **balance**, a **strong musculature, sure-footedness, the ability to recognize and adjust to outside conditions** (think wire tension, wind, etc.), and

flexibility. These would be considered the **hard skills**, knowledge, and physical abilities that Lijana needed to complete the task at hand. Those she had in spades.

But what were the soft skills needed for her to complete her daunting task?

- She had **resilience**, the ability to come back from a failure with a positive attitude.
- She practiced **collaboration**, the willingness to reach out, and rely on her brother to complete the monumental task at hand.
- She was **emotionally steady**, not letting any of the hiccups that happened on the high wire (like hooking in her balancing pole incorrectly mid-walk), sway her goal of finishing her challenge.
- She was **empathetic** in her pursuit. It may seem strange, but Lijana was more concerned about her brother than herself, (as he was about her!), during the breath-taking trek. They were a team accomplishing the walk together, for and with each other.

All these traits are considered soft skills. Without them, regardless of her mastery of skywalking, Lijana would not have been able to reach her goal.

Both hard and soft skills are necessary to succeed in any given career, but in this present age, with the amount of knowledge and training available to us, the real skills gap is not found in the lack of schooling that people have when entering the workforce. The thing that is most lacking in their journey towards success is, you guessed it, soft skills!

When Linkedin CEO, Jeff Weiner, gave a keynote at Talent Connect 2018, he stated that from their poll of HR leaders, **the greatest skills gap was not found hard skills** (the technical abilities you possess), **but in soft skills** (the relational abilities you possess.)[3]

What really matters for success, character, happiness, and life-long achievements is a definite set of emotional skills – your EQ – not just purely cognitive abilities that are measured by conventional IQ tests.

— DANIEL GOLEMAN

Soft Skills and You

What do soft skills look like at work in the real world? Imagine you are a brilliant salesperson, knowing every strategy and tactic to employ. Your knowledge of your industry is amazing, and your work ethic is stellar... *but if you struggle to connect with your team or don't know how to engage and retain clients,* you will not be able to accomplish all that you could or should. Your hard skills need the support of your soft skills to meet your yearly sales goal.

Let's make it personal. Think about yourself and how you interact with the people that you work with right now.

- Who stands out above the rest?
- Who has the greatest influence in your workplace?
- Who has the ear of your manager?
- Who brings the team down with negativity?
- Who is an encourager and a team cheerleader?
- Who do you like working with?
- Who do you dread working with?
- Who makes it difficult for the team to meet deadlines?
- Who pushes everyone to do their best?

All these questions can be answered when you look at them through the lens of soft skills.

While the technical abilities that you need to achieve your job are highly important, your **character**, your **attitude**, your **ability to relate** to others, your **motivation** and **confidence**, and your **willingness to collaborate** can determine whether or not you move forward in your career.

Bruce Tulgan, author and soft skills expert, says, "**Today's best talent may show up as masters of the newfangled, with the latest and greatest methods. But what they are missing – way too often – are the "old-fashioned basics," or what is commonly referred to as soft skills.**"[4]

These relational super skills that managers long for and co-workers appreciate, **might be called soft skills**, but **their impact on your life and surroundings are anything but soft.** They are powerful and essential! The hard facts are that your soft skills abilities are directly linked to your ability to succeed.

In a recent article, Forbes stated that *94% of recruiting professionals say employees with stronger soft skills have a better chance of being promoted.*[5]

94%! That is a whole lot of folks who know what they are talking about, letting you know that soft skills are crazy important!

Let's get more personal. Answer these questions:

1. How do you comport yourself in business and with your colleagues?
2. How do you relate to your boss?
3. How do you show up as a team player?
4. How does your character shape your actions?
5. How does your attitude impact your co-workers?

The answer to these questions can and will determine how seriously you are taken in the workplace and how you will advance in your future.

How I Began Learning the Soft Skills Essentials

Early on in my career, as I was growing in the knowledge of the security industry (hard skills) and earning my bachelor's degree (hard skills), I was recognizing something different about my work ethic and my ability to relate with others. My tenacity and willingness (soft skills) to engage my customers, were impacting my sales, more than being able to navigate our sales system or learning new phone techniques. While no one in the industry was really talking about soft skills, their importance was playing out in my day to day connections within and without my company.

By trial and error, I was discovering truths that were impacting my ability to both sell and move forward in my industry. *And they had absolutely nothing to do with my ability to take finals or read books on sales strategies!*

- I found that if I was myself, true to my values, and honest about my abilities, my managers, co-workers, and clients were more willing to trust me.
- I found that if I built a relationship with my clients by showing them that I honestly cared about helping them, I established a relational foundation that would not just get me through the first sale, but one that would last for years (even when things didn't always go right!)
- I found that if I was tenacious and resilient and willing to work hard, even if I didn't have the "right" degree at the time, I was offered promotions because people liked working with me.

More than once, I was offered opportunities that superseded my hard skills (technical ability), because of my soft skills (character traits and interpersonal capabilities). My managers trusted me with more, not because of what degree

I had, but because I had proven myself to be a good communicator, a solid team member, and a hard worker.

This life-changing skills are the ones that you will get to explore in the following chapters! I can't wait to share the essentials I learned with you

Which Skills Are Essential?

You may be thinking, *if soft skills are so important, why didn't I learn about them in school?* Another great question! Maybe your professors thought that these skills were learned in living life... by osmosis. Maybe they thought as you were maturing as a young person and becoming an adult, that you would pick up these skills by trial and error. That may be true to some extent. Maybe your parents impressed upon you the importance of sharing, of being kind, and of being honest, both in big and small ways. Your teachers may have encouraged empathy, collaboration, and tenacity in the classroom. If you did, you have a head start in learning the essentials!

But the truth is, you are never done learning! Just like the technical skills that you acquired in college or at trade school or in your work life, these skills need to be practiced and developed. The same determination that you use to learn hard skills (such as the foundational experience of mastering keyboarding in elementary school) can translate to soft skills (the emotional experience of developing resilience in the workplace). You don't start out perfect. You practice. Then you practice. Then you practice some more.

Numerous soft skills can be explored. One website reported 135 different soft skills that you can list on your resume. *135?* I don't know about you, but that seems a little overwhelming to me.

In the next chapters, I will strip that list down to the **ten essentials needed to cross the soft skills gap. Ten essentials** to study, meditate on, practice, and build **(1 essential for each finger – an easy way to memorize them!)**

These essentials will build out your confidence and your resume at the same time. They will challenge your character and develop your work ethic. They are power skills that you can use each and every day to connect with those around you, building out important relationships. These skills translate across industries and companies and will be an asset to you wherever you go, whether you stay at your company for the next ten years or launch out building your own business empire.

Crossing the Gap

As you stand at that precipice looking into your future, know that you won't be traveling on a thread-like high-wire towards your destiny. (Phew!) In the following chapters, you will be crossing the gap between who you are and who you are meant to be, sure-footed and steady, on a firm foundation of soft skills, (a solid bridge!), built out by your practice, your diligence, and your discipline.

Your dreams, your goals, and your future are yours for the taking. The ten essentials will help get you there!

Stop clowning around and get ready to cross the gap!

ESSENTIAL #1: AUDACIOUS AUTHENTICITY

The greatest act of courage is to be and to own all of who you are – without apology, without excuses, without masks to cover the truth of who you are.

— DEBBIE FORD

In this chapter, we will be looking at the most foundational essential... what it means to be authentic. Audaciously authentic. No holds barred. All out. This is the first essential because it is the base that you will build all your other skills on. To find out what it means to be authentic, let's look at what it means to be inauthentic. It's time to meet a real, honest-to-goodness, non-creepy clown,

Joseph Grimaldi. He mastered the art of inauthenticity - of covering up his true self and fooling the world!

Who in the World is Joseph Grimaldi?

Joseph Grimaldi is known as the father of modern-day clowning. Born into a family of singers and entertainers in December of 1778, Grimaldi first appeared on stage at the age of four. Throughout his career, he was known for making people laugh... hard! When he joined the Covent Garden Theatre in 1806, he developed a new type of pantomime clown – part rascal/part buffoon. His signature look was the white face make-up that he donned each night. For the next decade at that theater, he perfected his stylized clowning. His silent antics made the crowds roar.[1]

Other types of clown personalities have developed down through the centuries as well. An "auguste" clown usually sports a red nose, small or large, has a dopey personality, and is the butt of all the jokes. A character clown is one that embraces a well-known profession, (think firefighter clowns in the *Dumbo* movie) to set up a clown gag. In each type of clowning, behaviors and costumes are over-exaggerated to heighten the humor of the situation. Clown gags parody real-life situations to the nth degree, with over the top situational comedy (diving into a bucket from a high dive or stuffing twenty-seven clowns in a car, anyone?). Hilarity and madness ensue.

But back to Grimaldi and his white face clown personae... his cultural influence was so great that other clowns began to mimic his antics and costumes. The clowns who copied his look and style were nicknamed "joeys" in his honor. The crowds adored Grimaldi. His comedic talent was unparalleled in that day, and his memoir was edited by none other than Charles Dickens (not bad for a clown, right?!). Grimaldi's painted face, the character he hid behind, was the mask he used to perpetuate his career. It served him well, and his look is still used in circus acts today.

What is Your Mask?

Unfortunately, crazy clown gimmicks and makeup don't translate well to the workplace. Over the top antics and exaggerated mannerisms can be off-putting, to say the least. I'm not talking about having fun or joy in the workplace. (That is the best part of working with a team!) I am talking about how you hide behind a "mask" and don't bring who you really are into your work. Or how you exaggerate your gifts or hide your flaws in hopes that others believe that is the real you. Braggadocio and false humility both, seldom ring true. The real question is: who are you right here, right now? Who is the "foundational" you?

Authentic:

true to one's own personality, spirit, or character

The reason that people often don't like clowns is that they don't know who is under all that makeup. If you want to become the person you are meant to be, you start by understanding who you are and then by bringing your most authentic self to the workplace. For you to cross the soft skills gap… **you are going to have to lose the mask.**

Don't Be a Joey

Obviously, no one is headed in to work with white face, giant shoes, or a red nose these days. (Which is good… because that would be weird.) But most people struggle with being authentic in the workplace. If you find it hard to reveal your true self to those you work with, you are not alone. It feels vulnerable to reveal yourself, your values, your weaknesses, and sometimes, even your strengths. There are a lot of reasons that you may "don the mask" in the office.

Sociologist Ervin Goffman says that in order to not feel vulnerable, "We cover. Covering [is] what happens when one feels one does not belong, feels vulnerable. We're afraid of how we might be perceived."[2] He concluded this is common in the workplace.

You may recognize this masking behavior in yourself.

- The person you are when you are with friends and family is entirely different than the person that you are at work.

- You try and portray perfection in the workplace, one without emotion or vulnerability.
- You don't want people to know that you fail on occasion or that you struggle with different skill sets (public speaking, cold calling, organization, strategies, procrastination... I could go on for days!)
- You are a people pleaser and are trying to live up to someone else's idea of who you should be (parents, professors, managers, etc.) In this case, they are the ones asking you to wear the mask.

Whatever the reason, you are covering up who you are. It is critical to recognize how powerful it is when you bring the fullness of who you are into your work.

Foundational You

Why is authenticity so crucial in crossing the soft-skills gap? **Who you are at the core, the foundational you, is the you that has the most impact on the world.**

You may think that you are not enough (or too much) just the way you are. But if you are not authentic, comfortable in your own skin, able to own up to your glorious strengths or your cringy weaknesses, you will often find yourself unfulfilled and unhappy. Why is that?

Character is the real foundation of all worthwhile success.

— JOHN HAYES HAMMOND

Think about this... **there is no one else in the world like you.** Truly. You are unique. Your experiences, your story, your gifts and talents, your struggles, and your weaknesses, are yours alone. You are doing this work that you are doing like no one else can. Your perspective, your thoughts, the words that you speak, can bring clarity in a different way than anyone else.

Take a moment and think about these two truths:

1. **If you are not honest about who you are, there is no point of true connection** between **yourself and others.**
2. **If you are not honest about who you are, you stunt the possibility for change and growth in your future.**

What Does A Mask Look Like?

Have you ever had a co-worker who brags endlessly about their skill set, their smarts, or their extraordinary abilities...

and yet their results don't match up with their bravado? (Super annoying, isn't it?)

Or on the other hand, have you ever had a colleague who puts themselves down, not owning up to their true worth, but they come through over and over again, caring about others, adding value to the team, and going above and beyond in their work? (This is also maddening!) Both of these behaviors are masks they have chosen to wear to cover up insecurity or lack of confidence and find acceptance with others. But neither type of behavior enables them to be or become all that they could be.

Real trust, in yourself and with others, is built when you know the strengths, weaknesses, and values in yourself and in those you work with. There is no hilarity involved when your co-workers and managers don't trust you or can't figure you out. And vice-versa. **When you wear a mask, thinking it hides your flaws or vulnerabilities, you are the one who is deceived.**

Know thyself.

— SOCRATES

What Authenticity Is Not

There are some misconceptions about authenticity... some folks think that being authentic means being uncensored in your attitudes or insensitive about how your words or choices affect others. This couldn't be further from the truth.

- Authenticity is not airing all your dirty laundry at work. (You want to maintain a professional, calm attitude and be able to manage your emotions. We will explore this with Essential #2.)
- Authenticity is not leading with a this-is-who-I-am-and-I-am-not-going-to-change-so-deal-with-it attitude. This kind of confrontational mindset actually literally puts you at odds with the idea that you can grow.
- Authenticity is not blurting out all your opinions or sharing what you think about any given subject at any time.

Think of authenticity as a character and skill set mirror that reflects who you truly are, what you believe, and your abilities, including both your shortcomings and your strengths. If you don't have a clear picture of who you are...it is very difficult to bring authenticity in the workplace.

The big question is, **do you know who you are (your values, strengths, and weaknesses?)**

Losing My Mask...Finding My Way

While pursuing my MBA at Webster University, I was nearing the end of my studies. With a full-time job taking up my day, I was getting a bit tired and looking for the best way to complete my electives with the least amount of work. (I love a good workaround!) While registering for classes, I noticed that there were three seminar courses that were worth one credit hour each. All I had to do was give up an entire Saturday for each seminar (a total of three Saturdays), and I would get credit for an elective course.

One of those Saturday classes was a Myers Briggs seminar.

Myers Briggs Type Indicator is a personality test based on Carl Jung's personality theory. There are eight different personality preferences that influence your behavior and choices.

Extraversion vs. Introversion. Sensing vs. Intuition.

Thinking vs. Feeling. Judging vs. Perceiving.

I had no idea what Myers Briggs was before taking the seminar. I was mesmerized by what I learned that day. I thought I was just going to knock my elective credits out of the way. But this test changed how I saw myself and my future. It focused my work and re-energized my efforts!

By answering a series of questions, the test indicates what personality type you are. There are sixteen different personality type combinations broken down into four different categories: analysts, diplomats, sentinels, and explorers. These categories each have four different subsets.[3]

1. **Analysts** – architect, logician, commander, debater
2. **Diplomats** – advocate, mediator, protagonist, campaigner
3. **Sentinels** – logistician, executive, defender, consul
4. **Explorers** – virtuoso, adventurer, entrepreneur, entertainer

The results of the type indicator can be used to show your strengths, weaknesses, and preferences. It can help determine how you work best with others, what careers are a good fit for you, and what your leadership skills tend to be.

Keep in mind...there is no "best type." This test is simply a mirror of your preferences, skills, and thought processes – showing you who you are.

I tested as an ENTJ (Extraversion. Intuition. Thinking. Judging.) under the Sentinel category as an Executive.

Neris Analytics, a company that administers and analyzes the test, states that, "Executive personalities lead by example, demonstrating dedication and purposeful honesty, and an utter rejection of laziness and cheating, especially in work."

I was amazed at how accurate the profile was of my typical behaviors! I felt like someone was peering into my brain and pulling out my thoughts and practices. The test results validated that my years of study were focused on the right topics since I naturally behaved as an executive. (PHEW!)

This was not just important to me professionally but personally. In my early years of corporate work, I would take on any mask/identity that was needed to get the job done. It wasn't until my experience with the Myers Briggs survey course that my eyes were opened to the fact that I was designed with natural strengths and talents. **To be my best, I needed to embrace that truth and run forward.**

I also realized I had been taking on identities projected by others as I was trying to be what I thought they wanted me to be. During that course, I found myself embracing authenticity. It was freeing! The experience incited me to find my true calling and purpose in my career.

This seminar was the most memorable course of all my studies. I went home and tried to figure out my wife's profile (along with any other close family member I could think of!) It was fun and amazing, realizing that each and every person is completely different. This realization not only unlocked the door to me knowing myself, but was key in helping me understand others, and embracing those unique differences. Everyone working in their foundational state together, in unified collaboration, is the thing that makes humankind great. (Recognizing this will be key when we talk about Essential #4 - Cohesive Collaboration!)

The DISC assessment discusses four reference points:

Dominance – direct, strong-willed and forceful

Influence – sociable, talkative and lively

Steadiness – gentle, accommodating and soft-hearted

Conscientiousness – private, analytical and logical

Several years later, I was introduced to the DISC assessment test from an employment screening. **DISC is an acronym that stands for the four different behaviors of dominance, influence, steadiness, and conscientiousness.**[4] This personality assessment focuses on your patterns of behavior. I found this assessment to be equally enlightening. My most dominant characteristic is **influence** – a quality that lends itself to thriving in an environment that includes the volatility and unpredictability of sales and management. I like people. I want to do whatever I can to help them. Those relationship-building skills enable me to connect with my managers and clients and get the job done.

People Keys, a behavioral analyst company that specializes in DISC assessment, states that, "I-personality styles are very talkative, enthusiastic, and optimistic. They thrive on fun experiences and being around other people. The I-style will talk to a complete stranger and is not afraid to be the center of attention. They tend to be both trusting and optimistic. Because they can get people on their side very quickly and can talk their way in and out of most things, the "I" style is known to be both persuasive and influential. They tend to be somewhat emotional and, at times, very spontaneous or impulsive."[5]

Knowing myself, my strengths and weaknesses, gave me a leg up in work, but also set the course for my personal growth. I wanted everyone I knew to get the benefit of knowing their "foundational" self. (You can tell I am passionate about this!)

In the summer of 2019, I joined the John Maxwell Team, a "leadership, coaching, speaking, and training development program." I was given the opportunity to become a certified behavioral assessment consultant with DISC. I jumped at the chance to utilize this skill for my own growth and the growth of others that I worked with.

I use my DISC certification as a mirror for others, bringing awareness to each person's own behavior, strengths, and weaknesses. With this mirror, the people I work with are learning in moments, what took years for me to discover on my own.

We are constantly invited to be who we are.

— HENRY DAVID THOREAU

Audaciously Authentic You

"I love being around that person at my office that is so fake and untrustworthy!" *said no one ever.*

The first step in your journey of authenticity is realizing the value of authenticity.

Authenticity is valuable because:

1. **Knowing who you are gives you a firm foundation upon which to build your life – both personally and professionally** (Think of building a house with

a solid foundation, knowing if you use excellence and care, that it will remain true and sound for years.)

2. **Authenticity allows you to acknowledge and develop your natural gifts and technical abilities** (Think of an athlete studying film of their last game and recognizing the plays and skills that worked so they can repeat and build off of those wins.)

3. **Authenticity grants you humility in recognizing your weaknesses, and gives you a template for growth.** (Think of that same athlete studying that film looking for ways to improve their game and rectify past errors.)

4. **Knowing your strengths helps you recognize the work you will excel at and the atmosphere you will thrive in** (i.e., if you are an introvert who is drained by people and chaos…maybe don't work on the stock market trade floor…just a thought.)

5. **Knowing your weaknesses helps you recognize the need for others, their strengths, and the power of collaboration** (Teamwork makes the dream work! We will explore this more with Essential #7.)

6. **Authentic people are drawn to, and like working with, other authentic people** (RELATIONSHIPS ARE KEY in succeeding in the workplace!)

7. **Authenticity helps you disregard the labels and masks that others want you to wear** (No matter how much your parents want you to be a doctor, if you can't tell a spleen from a duodenum? Please,

please, don't be a doctor. Stay in your lane. You can
be brilliant in a different way.)

How Do You Practice Authenticity in Your Life?

Bill George, Harvard Fellow, and author of *Authentic
Leadership* says that authentic leaders, "...don't hide behind
their flaws; instead, they seek to understand them. This
lifelong developmental process is similar to what musicians
and athletes go through in improving their capabilities."[6]

A lifelong developmental process. It is a good idea to take the
long lens approach when building out the ten essentials in
your own life. Practicing authenticity is a lifelong journey. It
is not something that happens overnight. You are continually
changing, growing, and learning. As you are becoming the
person you are meant to be, you have permission to take
your time in learning who you truly are, losing your mask,
and practicing authenticity.

Practice Authenticity:

- Take a personality assessment and discover your
  personality type. Learn more about who you are and
  how you function. This is key in learning more about
  your authentic self and how you can best work with
  others.

- (You can use this link (LINK HERE) to access the Stop Clowning Around DISC Assessment.)
- Take three to five people who are close to you, those who encourage you and are rooting for you and ask them to write a paragraph or two about who they perceive you to be. Does it line up with who you hope to be perceived as?
- Get away for some time by yourself. Visualize and write out (or draw pictures) of your perfect life. How would you live and act? What would you like to be doing in your career, in your family, with your hobbies, etc.? What relationships do you have and what do they look like? Be honest with yourself– It's only for you. Compare to where you are to where you want to be. How can being authentic move you toward your dream life?
- Sign a contract with yourself to keep integrity with yourself when tempted to jump off course and hide behind a mask.
- Spend time with your resume. What are the skills and gifts that are apparent in your work? What are the areas that you see need further development? What were the successes that you got where you are? By reviewing your past work, you can often find a clearer path for the future.
- Own up to your mistakes and weaknesses. Choose to learn from them rather than deny or ignore them. You become more approachable and relatable when you acknowledge your need for growth or help or both.

- Align your values with the organization that you represent. If you often disagree with policy or ethics at your company, recognize that you can't be authentic there. Find a workplace that embraces your core values.

Audacious authenticity is impactful. When you lose your mask and bring your foundational self to your work, your interactions, and your relationships, it allows others to do the same! Cool, right? So, there is only one thing left to do....

Stop clowning around and embrace audacious authenticity!

ESSENTIAL #2: EMOTIONAL STEADINESS

The key to success is emotional stability.

— WARREN BUFFET

Ladies and Gentlemen, Welcome to the Circus!

In case you didn't know, 1882 was a big year for the world. The germ that caused tuberculosis was discovered by a German scientist named Dr. Koch. Thomas Edison crafted the first string of Christmas lights (God bless him, everyone!). And most importantly, it was the year that P.T. Barnum bought his famed African elephant, Jumbo, from the London Zoo. The circus world would never be the same.

Jumbo, the seven-ton, thirteen-foot-tall pachyderm, sparked "Jumbo-mania" across the United States. As Barnum's traveling circus train rolled into towns across the country, Jumbo achieved rock-star status. His name became synonymous with anything larger-than-life. *Ever fly on a jumbo jet? Or eat a jumbo size meal?* You can thank Barnum's elephant for that!

As if this wasn't enough excitement, 1882 was also the year that Barnum added the third ring to his circus showcase. Three rings, folks! Up until 1872, circuses had primarily used a single ring.[1] The center ring was the biggest ring, showcasing the most spectacular animal acts, fearless tight rope walkers, stunning trapeze artists, and of course, the magnificent Jumbo. The side rings were occupied by supporting sideshows, keeping the audience entranced. There was so much to see that you couldn't take it all in!

Three rings meant more seats, more money, and more entertainment! Everything was bigger, brighter, shinier, and busier than before. **In fact, everything about the circus was over the top!** The music was fast and loud. The costumes were outrageous. The clown gags were beyond goofy. The ringmaster's voice, echoing through a giant megaphone, was loud and bellowing.

Exaggeration was the name of the game. Jumbo wasn't just a big elephant...he was the hugest...EVER. The circus wasn't just an evening of entertainment...THIS WAS THE GREATEST SHOW ON EARTH!

So, let me ask you this. **Have you ever felt like showing up to work on Monday morning is a whole lot like showing up to a three-ring circus?**

Your Own Personal Circus

Depending on where you work or who you work with, you might feel like you have your own gong show going on! Your work environment may be unstable, never knowing from day to day if lay-offs could occur. Your boss might blow up on occasion... or regularly. Your clients or customers have rock-star-like egos that need to be pandered to. Everything feels big and wild and out of control. (At least, out of your control.) You never really feel like you accomplish what you want or need to. Your success at work seems to wax and wane at the whims of those around you.

All the chaos? It's exhausting. So...

- How do you navigate a wild work environment where gossip rules and co-workers act out?
- How can you thrive in a space where the boss's own actions unleash chaos?
- How do you survive in an unstable environment without freaking out yourself?

Time to lean into Essential #2 – Emotional Steadiness!

The term **three-ring circus,** to mean an **out-of-control or chaotic situation,** first came into use at the turn of the twentieth century.

Working within a chaotic environment, or with chaotic people, can be draining and disheartening. When you find yourself being influenced by others' emotional outbursts or your company's instability for long periods of time, you can find yourself stressed-out and anxious, dreading the days ahead.

Emotional steadiness is an essential skill that can be developed over time. It can anchor you to a **rational state of mind.** It lends itself to **problem-solving,** instead of emotional outbursts. It focuses you on **reality** and gives you a way to cross the soft-skills gap in a circus-like environment - without becoming one of the over-the-top acts!

Figuring out how to maintain a calm and present attitude, no matter what is going on, can help you navigate the chaos around you.

Jumbo-Size Me!

Just like the circus is wildly exaggerated with its presentation, work-life can have the same qualities. People can over-hype whatever is going on around them. Humans tend to make decisions based on their emotions and react based on their feelings. Problems feel bigger, relationships seem crazier, stress can loom large, depending on what you tell yourself about your situation. There is the off chance that you could be over-exaggerating...just a little. The problem with over-exaggerating the conditions around you is that you can actually believe your own hype. Maybe you have entertained jumbo-sized thoughts in your own head.

This is the worst place I have ever worked.
The company is going down, and I am going down with it.
If I blow this deal, my career is over.
My boss hates me and is working against me.

Each of these statements is over-exaggerated, stress-inducing, worst-case-scenario. If these are actually true, how can you deal with them without having an emotional breakdown?

Over-Exaggerate Much?

One of the main ways that you can begin your journey of emotional steadiness is by recognizing over-exaggerated thoughts that you are telling yourself. You can also identify the hyped-up personalities of those around you.

You don't have room for over-exaggeration in your life. As a clown, over-exaggerating is a high calling. The bigger the pants? The greater the fall? The funnier the gag. The better the laugh. But you are not a clown. And your workplace isn't the circus. Jumbo-sized over-exaggeration is highly over-rated.

When you stop clowning around, you make the decision to NOT buy into over-exaggeration anymore. You are in the business of anchoring yourself to reality....you become a fact finder. **Knowing what is true, what is real, allows you to engage your calm, rational, problem-solving side** (vs. your fight or flight-I-just-want-to-survive mode) You can choose to speak the truth to yourself and remain calm, instead of adding to the chaos by freaking out. Sounds good, right?

Over-exaggeration starts with a kernel of truth... and then goes nuts. Let's look at the statements above again. How are they over-exaggerated?

This is the worst place in the world to work.

It might not be a great place to work, that is true. You may not enjoy the work, your supervisor ... or your co-workers. But consider all the jobs in the ENTIRE WORLD. Is your job the worst? Probably not.

The company is going down, and am I going down with it.

Your company may be going through a rough patch financially or corporately. It may even close at some point. Both of those things could be true. But is it closing tomorrow? Is your career and life's purpose linked solely to one company? Are you out of all foreseeable options? Probably not.

If I blow this deal, my career is over.

Blowing a deal with a client is a great disappointment. It may even impact your job. But does your entire career, all the effort you have put in over the years, and all of your relationships that you have nurtured in your work, hinge on one, single deal? Probably not.

My boss hates me and is working against me.

You may not get along with your boss. Different personalities can grate against each other. In some cases, a tricky relationship can affect your career. But does your boss hate you? Does he/she spend hours plotting your demise? Is your boss's greatest joy finding out ways to torment you? Probably not.

What is the reality of your situation? When you take a deep breath and assess your current problem with your work, co-worker, or boss, **what are you really dealing with? Are you over-exaggerating? Or are you stripping away those high-flying emotions of yours and sticking to the truth?**

It's time to find out the facts and bring a little calm to your three-ring circus. Much of workplace anxiety comes from forecasting worst-case scenarios THAT COULD HAPPEN... but haven't happened yet. And may never happen.

Be present. What is actually going on in your life TODAY? This is the first truth that you can build your emotional steadiness on.

Live in the now.

— GARTH, *WAYNE'S WORLD*

Freaking Out vs. Finding Out The Facts

Stripping down over-exaggerated facts to the stark truth helps to alleviate irrational fears. Once you know the truth of the situation, you have a clear picture of what you are dealing with, and you can determine how you should proceed with emotional steadiness. The opposite of emotional steadiness is freaking out. Ever been around someone who freaks out regularly? It is unsettling—both for the person freaking out and the people surrounding them.

Get your facts first, then you can distort them as much as you please.

— MARK TWAIN

Recently, I was dealing with a vendor who blew up. Not in a good way. This vendor was not happy with how our company had installed our product for them. Even though I had not personally installed our company product at the job site, I was the relationship manager... so I was the person who got yelled at. Not the best way to start your day. Welcome to my three-ring-circus!

I had a choice of how I could respond to the vendor, to the situation, and to our company.

1. I could join in the vendor's frustration, freak out, rail against our company, and yell at the person who installed the product incorrectly.
2. I could remain calm, find out the facts, be empathetic with the person who messed up (because we all make mistakes!), and move forward with a plan to solve the problem for our vendor.

I chose option B.

Why? **Because emotional steadiness breeds emotional steadiness.** If I want to build calm, respectful business relationships, I need to be calm and respectful. If I want to experience a peaceful workplace, I need to be a peaceful person. If I want people to be empathetic and listen to me instead of yelling at me, I need to be an empathetic listener. If I want to problem-solve creatively, I need my mind to be clear and my emotions to be kept in check. This calm state helps me move forward and help our vendor resolve the issue at hand.

Have you ever noticed when your boss freaks out... that the freaking out impacts everyone? Just as their emotions influence you, your emotions influence those around you.

For good. Or bad. I suggest using your calm, problem-solving brain for good. (Just a suggestion, of course.)

You Decide

In a 2019 Stanford study, "Beyond Emotional Similarity: The Role of Situation Specific Motives," research showed that depending on how people are motivated, they can choose to respond differently than the emotions being displayed around them. Alex Shashkevich of the Stanford News Service reported that, "Their study found that when a person wanted to stay calm, they remained relatively unfazed by angry people, but if they wanted to feel angry, then they were highly influenced by angry people."[2] Amazing!

This is actually fantastic news! It means… **you decide how you act in any given situation.** You are NOT held hostage by the chaos around you, whether it is coming from corporate upheaval, a frantic co-worker, or an unmotivated supervisor. YOU DECIDE how you will respond today, tomorrow, and in the future.

So…what is your motivation?

Do you want to be angry, stressed-out, whipped-up, and exhausted?

or

Do you want to be calm, un-ruffled, focused, and emotionally steady?

You decide.

Stress Reliever

In choosing to be emotionally steady, you are marrying your foundational self, the true you, with the behavior that you want to exhibit in stressful situations. Stress is a universal issue. But everyone experiences it differently.

The American Institute of Stress states that, "Stress is a highly personalized phenomenon and can vary widely even in identical situations for different reasons."[3] What you consider to be a "three-ring circus," could be someone else's walk in the park.

Think back to your DISC analysis – different personalities deal with situations in various ways. You may be thinking, *I am type A! I eat stress for breakfast! Or I worry for a living. I don't have a calm bone in my body.* This may be true. But remember, whatever natural behaviors you lean into, you can CHOOSE to lean into emotional steadiness when you ask yourself these two questions:

1. What do I know?
2. What can I do?

Let's apply those questions to two of the over-exaggerated statements above. Add your own answer, if it applies.

This is the worst place I have ever worked.

What do I know?

- I know that I have a job and I am supporting myself and my family.
- I am a resilient person and have skillfully navigated a difficult work environment.
- I am learning new skills and thought processes every day.

What can I do?

- I can identify why this job is so difficult and what could be done to improve it.
- I can come up with solutions to the problems I see and implement them or share them with leadership.
- If I am truly dissatisfied, I can look for a different job and work on my resume.

If I blow this deal, my career is over.

What do I know?

- This deal is important to my company and to me.
- I am a hard worker and always put my best efforts forward.
- My career is not dependent on one business deal.

What can I do?

- I can give my best effort and be diligent in my work on this deal.
- I can ask for input from others who are knowledgeable and give good advice.
- I can give myself permission to fail and learn from my mistakes.
- (More on life-changing essential #10 later!)

Practice Emotional Steadiness

What is an over-exaggerated statement you are currently telling yourself about your career or work life?

A jumbo-sized statement that I tell myself:

Break down the facts. What is the truth?

How is this statement over-exaggerated?

Answer the Emotional Steadiness questions.

What do I know?

What can I do?

. . .

This is what being emotionally steady feels like! You are using your skills and your knowledge, to move forward in a stressful situation. You can practice this emotional steadiness exercise throughout the day, at any time, in any situation. Use it to calm your nerves, to re-focus your thoughts, and move you forward.

Keep calm and carry on.

— BRITISH MINISTRY OF INFORMATION
WORLD WAR II

As you move forward, developing your own emotional steadiness, let these 5 truths anchor your journey:

1. Knowing what is true, what is real, allows you to engage your calm, rational, problem-solving side. (Hello, emotional steadiness!)
2. Emotional steadiness breeds emotional steadiness. Your actions and reactions influence others.
3. You are not held hostage by the chaos around you.
4. YOU DECIDE how you act in any given situation.
5. No matter what behavior (worry, anxiety, fear) you naturally lean into, YOU CAN CHOOSE to lean into emotional steadiness.

Practice Emotional Steadiness:

- Create a morning routine focused on mental and physical health to prepare yourself for the day. Exercise. Be quiet or still. Pray and meditate. Read for inspiration. Take deep breaths. Visualize the day.
- Journal your thoughts about your situation and work through the emotions of them until you feel satisfied that you know the truth.
- Hire a coach or therapist to assist you with life obstacles or emotional issues that you have.
- Take a nature hike. If you are able, move your office outdoors. Nature has a way of calming and bringing clarity.
- Look at anxiety-filled situations from a future view. In a year, will this decision be remembered or even important? Typically, you will find that most anxiety-filled decisions are not all that life-impacting.

Stop clowning around and lean into emotional steadiness!

ESSENTIAL #3: AVID CURIOSITY

Never lose a holy curiosity.

— ALBERT EINSTEIN

My Ticket Of Entry

When I started my rather non-illustrious junior college career after high school, I really hated all my core classes… English, history, math. I was tired of them. I had just taken all of those classes the year before. Why did I have to take them over again for college? (No, really… why did I? I think college education should be focused on the degree niche…but that is another book entirely!) Needless to say, my first foray into college learning was uninspiring. I was uninterested. Bored. Less than curious.

Ironically, when I went back to college three years later and fell in love with business and management, I had to take college algebra over...because I had failed it my first time through. But there was a fundamental shift in my mindset. I was curious. I was excited to learn. I wanted to know more. I was able to see the "why" of how math could help in my career. My learning had purpose. It made sense to me. I finished the course with an A. Sometimes students just need to see the purpose behind learning. That spark of curiosity needs to be re-ignited.

Throughout my lengthy college and graduate school career, my curiosity was piqued continuously because I was learning about subjects that I was interested in. The monotony of schoolwork was overshadowed by the fact that I was learning things that were impacting my life. I was finding out about the mechanics of business. I was delving into leadership techniques. I was putting new communication skills into daily practice. Since I was working and going to school at the same time, I was able to apply the lessons I was learning in school on the job. I was growing. I was increasing my knowledge. Learning became fascinating. I also felt sure that once I finally had my MBA in hand, new doors of opportunity would be flung open to me. Because... a degree means something!

Imagine my surprise when I graduated! Promotions didn't come pouring in. No one threw me a "You-got-your-MBA" party. This was a big life lesson. While it was necessary to earn my degree to keep moving forward in my career, **my degree wasn't a guarantee for success. It was merely my ticket of entry.** It got me into the show, but I had to keep learning and growing in my knowledge to stay fresh and relevant in my work. My learning journey was my responsibility... no one else's. **The truth is that my professional growth journey won't end... until I do.**

The Curiosity Key

The bonus is... I love learning now! My younger self would be amazed... I was a mediocre student at best. Now, you rarely find me without a book I'm reading, or listening to a riveting podcast, or talking to someone knowledgeable in their practice or field. I find that talking to people about what they know fuels my own curiosity. (I have my CEO's number on speed dial!) **The key to my love of learning? I am super interested in the things I am learning about.**

When I talk to leaders and influencers, I feel like I am discovering powerful secrets. When I interview people about their careers, I am getting insight into a new world. When I download a new podcast, I am invited into someone else's sensibility. The more I learn, the more ideas are sparked in me. I am pretty much an idea generator at this point.

. . .

Curiosity... And More Curiosity

Learning about DISC, figuring out my own behavior type, and getting certified was a natural learning leap for me. It came from being hopelessly curious about people. I am fascinated by what makes people tick. *Why do they respond the way they do? Why do they interact with others in a certain way? How do they make their decisions?* I am interested in people... their behavior, their thought processes, and how these processes move them forward in the world.

The funny thing is... the more I know about people... the more I realize I don't know. Curiosity lends itself to more wondering, more questioning, and more learning. The more I get to know how and why people behave, the more I realize that there are still worlds to discover. Uncovering new ideas and new ways to help people succeed is exciting. (Hello, curiosity!)

The King of Curiosity

Albert Einstein, physicist extraordinaire, was one of the most brilliant minds of the 20th century. **His curiosity was boundless.** Most folks have passing thoughts, but Albert would ruminate on his for years. This curious nature was ignited in childhood. As a young boy, Albert was thoroughly fascinated by the workings of the compass and by geometry. A physical science book given to him at the age of sixteen by his father's friend, ignited the wonder that Albert would ponder for decades, "What would it be like to ride alongside a beam of light?" This thought carried him into the 20th century.

Albert's young adult years were turbulent (dropping out of high school, re-locating to Switzerland to attend university, weathering parental disapproval over his star-crossed relationship with first wife, Mileva, trying to find employment without backing from his professors), he still stayed curious. Thinking. Pondering. Daydreaming about light.

Einstein read scientific papers. He studied advanced theories on his own. After graduating from university, without recommendations from his professors, he couldn't land a teaching job. Instead, he found a job as a patent clerk in Zurich, Switzerland. In the office, Einstein would quickly finish his work and spend the rest of his workday imagining, thinking, and pondering his emerging theory of the speed of light.

In 1905, at the age of twenty-six, Einstein published four scientific papers that changed the course of modern physics. It took another nine years for Albert to carefully craft his magnum opus on the general theory of relativity. This theory launched his career. His discoveries about light, physics, and relativity are recorded in the annals of history. His imagination and his tenacity were unparalleled. **Einstein said of himself, "It's not that I'm so smart, it's just that I stay with problems longer."**[1] Curiosity is a powerful thing.

Einstein's willingness to stay curious changed science, history, and the world. My curiosity has led me down a different learning path. Where has your curiosity led you?

How Curious Are You?

So, my question to you is… what are you curious about? What grabs your interest? What practices make you lose yourself for hours in the wonder of discovery? What do you enjoy talking about **with** others? What do you want to know more about?

List five things that interest you and explain why they spark your imagination.

Now… ask yourself these questions:

- How often do you find yourself ruminating or daydreaming about these things?
- How can you cultivate curiosity in your daily routine?
- Are the things that you are curious about incorporated into your work life?

Curiosity has a way of opening doors and flipping on lights. "A-ha" moments happen when you get curious. Maybe you have even had one while reading this chapter!

. . .

Your Ticket Of Entry

The need for learning and curiosity doesn't stop when you walk the line in your college graduation ceremony or get your certificate from a trade school or get the promotion you have been working towards. **Your degree, your hard skill set, your abilities and talents, those are merely your ticket of entry.** You paid the price to get into the show. **You are responsible for your own learning journey.** If your company offers you workshops, in-house learning, or tuition re-imbursement, jump on that! (My company's education program allowed me to graduate debt-free.) But don't expect it!

Henry Kissinger said, "**Each success only buys an admission ticket to a more difficult problem.**"[2] In other words, with each achievement (graduation, certificate, promotion, deal) there is another hurdle, another struggle, or another opportunity for learning waiting for you. **It is up to you to keep learning and to keep building out the skills that you need to succeed and thrive in your career.** Your natural curiosity plays a huge role in that. The best part is? When you key into the type of work that you were meant for, learning becomes fun!

Your Beautiful Brain

You may be thinking in this moment, I'm no Einstein. (That makes two of us.) Maybe you feel like you aren't great at learning, I have amazing news for you. **You were made to**

learn. It is what your brain is designed for. Literally. The study of the brain has changed drastically in the last thirty years. It was once thought that after you reached adulthood your brain could not change. Neuroscientists have since been diving into the study of neuroplasticity. **Neuroplasticity is the capacity of the brain to develop and change throughout life, something Western science once thought impossible.**

Brainworks, pioneers in the field of neurofeedback and brain training technologies say it this way, "With every repetition of a thought or emotion, we reinforce a neural pathway - and with each new thought, we begin to create a new way of being. These small changes, frequently enough repeated, lead to changes in how our brains work."[3]

This is powerful stuff, right? Simply put, with the repetition of thoughts, you have the ability to change your brain! You can learn new ideas, practice new skills, and think differently about the world around you, strengthening those brain connections. Every time you get curious, start pondering and ruminating, your neurons (you have 86 billion in your brain!) are firing like crazy, creating stronger neural pathways.

Absolutely everyone can get better at virtually anything.

— DR. MICHAEL MERZENICH, THE "FATHER" OF NEUROPLASTICITY

Let's think about neuroplasticity in terms of Einstein. Just how curious was he about light? How many repeated thoughts did he have about gravity? How many times did he think about relativity? How was his brain changing as he pondered the universe and its laws?

Now let's think about neuroplasticity in terms of you.

- Just how curious are you about the things that interest you?
- How are you changing your brain as you learn about the things that you are passionate about?
- How does this change your outlook on your work?
- How does this impact your belief about your learning journey?

Maybe, like me, you were a mediocre student at best. Maybe you struggle to learn and that has put you off being curious. **The crazy thing is that you can actually change the way that you think about learning... to help you learn better.** How is that for being meta?

The important thing is to not stop questioning.

Curiosity has its own reason for existing.

— ALBERT EINSTEIN

Growth Mindset vs. Fixed Mindset

Carol Dweck, Stanford professor and author of *Mindset: The New Psychology of Success*, has studied people's ability to learn for decades. She says that, "**Individuals who believe their talents can be developed (through hard work, good strategies, and input from others) have a growth mindset.** They tend to achieve more than those with a more fixed mindset (those who believe their talents are innate gifts)."[4]

Here's the thing. If you tell yourself that you can't learn or that you don't need to learn (because you have so many amazing gifts and talents), that is a **fixed mindset**. Fixed mindsets are centered around not being curious, not asking questions, not trying new things, or not trying them long enough. Growth mindsets are centered around being curious, asking questions, trying new things, and being willing to practice them long enough to actually get good at them.

For example, I am pretty good at selling. I've done a lot of it over the years. I have built my career off of my knowledge and best practices.

A **fixed mindset** would tell me,

- I'm good. I don't need to learn anything else about selling. I know it all.
- I am not capable of learning the new software or systems involved in selling. I'm fine staying in my comfort zone.
- I should just stick with what I know and not try out new techniques or strategies.

A **growth mindset** would tell me,

- I'm good, but I can be better.
- I can learn new strategies.
- I can acquire new techniques.
- New technology might challenge me, but if I apply myself, I can eventually master it.

Growth mindset says here is always more to learn!

As you get curious, embrace a growth mindset. Start reframing the way that you see yourself as a learner. Change the statements that you make to yourself about your own abilities. Remind yourself that you actually have the power to change the way you think about learning and that you have the ability to learn (because neuroplasticity!). Find that thing (or five) that you are passionate about and start repeatedly thinking about it! Then put action to your thinking and start incorporating new techniques or moves or strategies.

Expect Some Bumps Along The Road

Remember that mistakes are a part of the learning process. When you start incorporating a new strategy or tool, remember you will probably stink at it at the beginning. Picture a baby falling while learning to walk... this baby is not a failure. This baby is a learner. A 12-month-old baby, newly walking, is shaky at best. They usually have a nice bruise or two on their forehead. They look more like lurchers than walkers. It's literally what the word toddler means. Give that baby a year and then just try to catch him as he runs from you in the park! One year from novice to expert.

In your own learning journey, expect some hiccups. Expect some falls. Then, keep trying. Find that thing you are passionate about, and you're on your way to finding your own learning niche – an area that you excel in! You can go from novice to expert (give yourself more than a year!) With curiosity, and with learning, you start becoming the person you are meant to be.

> You are going to suck. You're going to suck real bad at first. What you're going to find over time though is that eventually, you're going to suck less. And, eventually, you will suck so little that you're actually good.
>
> — GARRET J. WHITE, WARRIOR PROJECT

What Is A Learning Niche?

The reason I am successful at what I do is because…I love it! I love learning about what makes people tick. I enjoy meeting people's needs in creative ways. I thrive in situations when I have to come up with creative solutions for problems that present themselves. I like figuring out workarounds in tricky situations. I am fulfilled by mentoring young people. I love learning from those who have more years under their belt than I do. Is there something new I can learn in one of these areas? I'm in. My job is sales. My learning niche... is helping people.

If you are bored out of your mind and not the least bit curious about what is required of you at work, you may be in the wrong field. Maybe you haven't found your learning niche yet. A learning niche is an area of learning that you are passionate about, one that keeps you curious, motivated, and wanting to learn more.

Einstein's was light. Mine is people. What is yours?

Everybody is a genius. But if you judge a fish by its ability to climb a tree, it will live its whole life believing that it is stupid.

— ALBERT EINSTEIN

No Two Niches Look Alike

Several years ago, I had my car in the shop to get a repair done. The man that came to help me was a bit disheveled and greasy from the work he was already doing. In the off-handed way that we humans sometimes do, I judged him. I did a mental run-through comparing our intelligence, our net-worth, and how much better my life was than his. (Remember, I knew nothing about this guy.)

Then I had one of those epiphanies. The kind that knock you upside the head. As he shared his knowledge about my car and what needed to be done, it became clear that while I might be more intelligent than him in business, he was much more intelligent than I was when it came to mechanics and automobiles. I didn't have the least idea of how to accomplish what he said needed to be done. I needed this guy and his smarts!

I also noticed that this scruffy gentleman was happy. Keep in mind that I know many so-called high earners that are completely miserable. My mechanic friend had found his niche! His skill set, his brain, his curiosity, had led him to this place of excellence. It was clear this guy was passionate about his work.

I took a step back that day and recognized that no one is "smarter" than anyone else. We are all smart in certain categories, and we can all learn from each other. This interchange deeply influenced how I view others. I am trying to judge differently! Now I am intentional about being genuinely interested in others. I ask questions that allow me to learn from them and about them. What I have found is that I learn more from diverse people than I ever would from reading more books or watching videos.

A few questions to ponder....

1. What do you think your learning niche is?
2. Are you developing your interests in this area? If so, how?
3. Does your current work fit in this niche? If not, what kind of work would pique your curiosity?

Practicing Avid Curiosity

Curiosity is essential in crossing the skills gap. It lends itself to creativity, problem-solving, and achieving excellence in your hard skills. It enables you to learn and grow and then grow some more.

Take some time after this chapter to practice curiosity. Here are some ideas for building out this skill.

- Prepare a list of things/categories you would like to grow in. Choose one and pursue it by reading about it, taking a class or joining an interest group.
- Compile a list of books that are of interest in a topic you wish to grow in and map out a reading plan for this next year.
- Watch videos (YouTube is full of valuable free information) on your chosen topic of growth.
- Find experts in your topic of growth seek permission to interview and learn from them.
- Go to a seminar or enroll in an online webinar related to your topic of growth.
- Join a mastermind of like-minded individuals and immerse yourself with the people living it out your passion.

Stop clowning around and get curious!

ESSENTIAL #4: RELATIONAL DEVELOPMENT

Spend more time with people who bring out the best in you, not the stress in you.

— *ANONYMOUS*

W e Love You, GPS!

It is hard to imagine a world without GPS, isn't it? NASA's global positioning system, initially designed for tracking nuclear submarines during the Cold War, now gently directs all your comings and goings from places unknown to your chosen destination. (Clearly the more difficult task.)

GPS instructs you and guides through the wildness that is modern-day driving. (Speed trap ahead!) Let's be honest.

Most of us have a slight panic attack when our GPS is down or is giving incorrect information. We start asking our phones questions like "Where are you sending me?" or "What the heck is wrong with you!???" GPS holds a firm grip on our sense of direction... and our sense of peace! We need it badly!

Stop Clowning Around GPS

In your life, professional development is a journey. You are trying to cross the skills gap and reach your destination. Your destination is the person you are meant to become. As you are navigating the trajectory of your career, you need a navigational system. Google Maps isn't going to cut it. You need a group of people who will advise you and keep you on the right path. In the likelihood that you make any missteps (which you will), their collective wisdom can take you down an alternate path to get you to your destination. You need them bad!

Think of Stop Clowning Around GPS not as a positioning system, but as **a professional development mandate:**

Get Peer Support!

Essential #4: Relational Development

Relational Development is all about you building out the team of people you want to help guide your professional development journey. It involves you aligning yourself with those around you who have the wisdom, work ethic, values, and character traits that you want to incorporate in your own life. Relational development influences your choices in who you invest time in and who you choose to let invest in you.

The people you surround yourself with influence your behaviors, so choose friends who have healthy habits.

— DAN BUETTNER

According to the *Harvard Business Review*, "**Studies show that social connections play a central role in fostering a sense of purpose and well-being in the workplace.**"[1] Workplace relationships are critical to your professional development journey. Solid friendships will build you up and enrich your work experience.

The relationships that you invest in will shape your future. When you choose to develop certain relationships, you choose a path. Where they lead, you follow... and vice versa. Investing in your support team can actually change the course of your life... and change you!

Jonah Berger, professor at the Wharton College of the University of Pennsylvania, says, "There's lots of research on something called **social facilitation**. Merely biking with someone else, for example, makes you bike faster. Running with someone else makes you run faster. Swimming with someone else makes you swim faster. Others can help us do things that we might not do otherwise. So, **we can set up situations where we actually encourage ourselves to be healthier, encourage ourselves to make better choices, by shaping our environment through others.**"[2]

Remember how your mom was so concerned about your friends in high school? She knew a thing or two! The people you hang out with shape your choices, your behaviors, your outlook, and, ultimately, your success! You become like the people you hang around with. And they become like you. It is fascinating to know the trajectory of your life is shaped by the people you surround yourself with. **What are your peeps facilitating in you right now?**

Entrepreneur Jim Rohn says, **"You are the average of the five people you spend the most time with."** List the five people you spend the most time with.

How are their behaviors and attitudes impacting you? How are they impacting your career and your success? How are they shaping the trajectory of your life?

Now. Let's be clear. **You can and should be friendly with everyone in your place of work.** But the relationships that you choose to develop (and it is your choice!) will directly impact your outlook on life, your work ethic, your values, and your career path. **Think about the qualities that you are trying to develop in yourself by reading this book. Do the people who surround you embody these ten essentials?** Because the best way to incorporate them into your own life is by hanging out with folks who are already practicing these skills.

Show me your friends and I'll show you your future.

— MARK AMBROSE

Who Are You Following?

The flip side of this is… don't invest a lot of time in relationships that will keep you from becoming the person you are meant to be. Think about it long and hard before spending extra time with colleagues who are unsupportive, mean, lazy, or negative. Why? Because the more time you spend with them…the more you become like them. If you have a lame support team that criticizes you, tears you down, or constantly complains, it will be a roadblock in your own development.

Who's more the foolish? The fool, or the fool who follows him?

— OBI-WAN KENOBI, *STAR WARS*

Following the Clowns

There is a famous circus clown gag involving a tiny car. A tiny car arrives in the circus ring. The door is flung open. One hundred seventeen clowns exit the car the size of Mini-Cooper. They just keep coming...and re-entering the car from the other side. The endless cycle of crazy clowns never stops!

It is ironic how this gag can seem to mirror the modern workplace. There seems to be an endless supply of folks who are going in circles. (Or going nowhere!) They are distracting. They lack focus and direction. And they don't seem to accomplish much. Have you met any of them? **They are the Socializers, the Gossipers, the Complainers, and the Antagonizers.**

The Socializers are good communicators, but they are more about chatter than problem-solving, brainstorming, or team building. Don't get me wrong. Socializers are the life of the party. It's just that the party life isn't going to help you become the person you are meant to become.

If you spend your hours socializing, you aren't putting your best into your work. This affects your performance, your ability to grow, and even your promote-ability. Don't let mindless chatter de-rail you from your goals. Keep focused. Keep moving ahead.

The Gossipers take it to another level. They are socializers with a side of snark. These folks seem to know all the business... about the business. They draw you into their web of rumors about the company and your colleagues, leaving you distracted and unfocused. (Do you ever wonder what they are saying about you?) Listening to gossip can leave you unsettled and uncertain, affecting your outlook about your work and life.

If you really have concerns about your company, your manager, or your co-workers? Go to the source. Sit down and have a heart to heart with that person. Find out the truth. Leave the gossip to the clowns. Don't engage. Walk away.

Next are **The Complainers**. You may have met one (or seven) of them on the job. Now, these could actually be some of the most focused and hard-working folks you will meet... they focus on how dissatisfied they are with their lives and are working hard to let everyone know about it! Their negativity is never-ending. They complain about everything from their managers and their workload to their personal lives and their paychecks. These folks seem to suck all the good air out of the room.

Life is not perfect... that is a given. But if you join in with the complaining, you will get trapped in that state of dissatisfaction, too. (Not the good kind!) Don't get stuck in a negative space. Get back on track to becoming the person you are meant to be.

And lastly, I give you The **Antagonizers**. Another well-known circus gag pits the clowns against the master of ceremonies. The master plays the heavy, trying to keep order. The clowns do their best to sabotage his authority, wreaking havoc and making fun of him. As usual, what is hilarious in a show isn't nearly as funny in real life.

The Antagonizers see the boss as the enemy. (The Socializers, Complainers and Gossipers can all fall into this category if they feel the boss challenging their unprofessional behavior). All these behaviors undermine the calm of the office, but when you view your boss as your enemy, it can undermine your career. You need positive interactions with your management to keep growing in your career. And your boss needs you to flourish in your position for the benefit of all around you.

The truth is… a good boss is not the heavy. While no boss is perfect (which is great because neither are you!), a good boss is on your side, cheering you on. When you are succeeding, growing, and killing it at work this is a win/win situation. (I'll share more about this later.)

Any fool can criticize, condemn and complain – and most fools do.

— BENJAMIN FRANKLIN

Here's the thing. You are going places. And you are smart. Don't let the clowns in the office get you off track. Surround yourself with people that you like, that are also going places, places you want to go too.

Include trusted leaders in your support team. *Is there a manager that impresses you with their ability to relate to others? Or a colleague in a higher position than you who is willing to share their business acumen?* These people might not be your peers, but their wisdom and skill sets can still help shape and motivate you in your journey.

Adopt-A-Leader

In my younger years, I struggled to find my place in the business world. At times I fell in with the socializers and listened to the gossipers and complainers. But I began to recognize that were certain leaders I admired and was drawn to. I could tell where their values met their work ethic. I wanted to emulate those honest, hardworking, trustworthy leaders. I wanted a good relationship with my managers. I quit following the clowns and started listening to the ringmasters... leaders within my team and company.

The people I held in high regard weren't threatened by me or my sales abilities. They wanted to help me. They shared their wisdom with me. They saw my success as a benefit to them and to our company. And they knew the biggest secret of all. **If we all are at our best... growth and work flourishes.**

Now, I adopt any leader willing to invest in and mentor me. They help me learn lessons quicker than I can on my own. If you want to fast track your success, adopt a leader. Hang out with those who are willing to inspire and help you.

If you cannot see where you are going, ask someone who has been there before.

— J. LOREN NORRIS

There are four types of leaders that can help you on your journey of professional development: **a good boss, a trustworthy mentor, a wise advisor, and an honest coach.**

A Good Boss

A good boss will give you space to grow and give you constructive criticism in your daily work. They can give you pointers that will make you more effective in your position. All you have to do is let them know you are interested in their input. Any good boss understands that his success is really based on the success of his people. Utilize their wisdom and insight. Ask your boss to help you improve in an area you want to grow in.

Wisdom of the Master

My first sales role was with ADT in Chicago. I noticed that some other big winners were spending evenings in the office. I adopted the same practice. I worked in the field, finding new business by day and spent the night planning and completing paperwork. It worked. I became one of the top performers on the team.

Luckily, I had an observant boss who decided to challenge the path I was taking. (GPS!) One day he stood by my cubical and said, "Scott, you are doing a good job." I swelled with pride. Then he said, "But as much as you work, anyone could be successful." My pride bubble burst. "You need to learn to work smarter and be more effective. The really great ones put up your numbers in half the time." He was right. I knew that by him taking the time to talk to me, he cared about me and my future. He saw my potential. His words caused me to re-evaluate how I spent my time. To this day, I'm always looking for ways to increase productivity.

My boss was not my enemy. He was not looking for ways to fire me. He was looking to make me better. He knew my success and happiness equaled success for him. He helped re-direct me on my journey.

A Trustworthy Mentor

A trustworthy mentor is not just someone who cares about the bottom line of your company, but someone who cares about the bottom line of your character. They are invested in seeing you develop as a whole person. A mentor is mature, someone who has travelled the path of business before you and can offer encouragement and insight along your journey. You are able to be completely honest with them, trusting them with your hopes and dreams. They keep that goal in mind as they advise you and spend time with you.

A great mentor will help bring people and resources together to help you overcome fears. Let me know if you find one.

— RICHIE NORTON

I have had several mentors throughout my own journey. Each person has been willing to spend time investing in me, meeting up for coffee, chatting on the phone, or answering my e-mails. For this reason, I love taking time to mentor those coming up behind me. I know how impactful these relationships have been in my own life.

A Wise Advisor

A wise advisor is someone who has keen knowledge and insight into your industry. While they might not spend in-depth time mentoring you, their advice is invaluable. They are a resource for you to bounce your ideas off of during critical moments in your journey. I have three advisors I turn to for insight in my life. I use them all as sounding boards in my decision-making process.

Ryan is a safe person who has a wide perspective. He knows what is going on in my organization. He brings value to every conversation we have and shows me the way as I move forward. Alan is more conservative in his approach. He is very detail-oriented and slow to take risky action. He brings a very calm and measured perspective to my life. Shawn has a doctorate and is a company owner. He shows maturity and wisdom with his advice and encourages me when we talk. I trust them implicitly.

An Honest Coach

At different intervals of my career, I have hired a professional coach to help me navigate my journey. A coach offers accountability, much like a personal trainer. You're working with them to build out the right path, and they keep you on track. A coach keeps a professional distance. Their purpose is not to become your best friend, but to challenge you in the areas that you want to grow in. They aren't afraid to speak the truth, in order for you to reach your goal. By hiring a coach, you are investing in your future.

A Greater Circle Of Influence

When you are building out your support team, recognize the critical role that curiosity plays in how you are influenced. You can be mentored or influenced by people that you don't even know by reading or watching or listening to them online.

Books, webinars, conferences and podcasts can shape you and be a part of your journey. With learning, you increase your circle of influence (support team + learning). Your circle of influence inspires you to be better. Virtual mentors can be authors, businesspeople, industry leaders, or conference speakers. (My virtual mentors would include Napolean Hill, Frank Bettger, John Maxwell, and more!). These people speak into your life and challenge you to improve in areas of career excellence and personal growth.

You may not have access to these people personally, but reading a book or listening to an interview, is like getting a sit-down with their brain, their processes, and their wisdom.

Pay It Forward

As you practice relational development, remember that great relationships take time to mature. They take an investment of time and energy. Know that when you take the time to build out important relationships and develop your circle of influence, your life will be richer. The same is true when you invest in those coming along behind you. Don't be afraid to teach and invest in those who look up to you. Be generous with your business secrets and wise counsel. Be the kind of mentor, listener, and encourager that you would like to have in your own life.

Practice Relational Development:

- Create a dream list of people you would like to meet, learn from, and work with. Discover ways to support/serve them so you can develop your relationship and be able to ask for help in the future.
- Surround yourself with people living what you desire to learn.
- Take an honest look at your current relationship circle. Dispose of negative relationships that are keeping you from pursuing your dreams and are not building you up.
- Ask your manager/supervisor to help you grow. Take their advice and follow up with how you implemented it. By putting action to their advice, you will get more coaching time as they recognize that you are not a time-waster.
- Ask a successful co-worker to help you grow by sharing some insights into their success. Follow through in the same way you did with your manager/supervisor.
- Invest in those coming up behind you. Take them out for coffee and share your knowledge.

Stop clowning around and choose relational development!

ESSENTIAL #5: EFFECTIVE COMMUNICATION

The single biggest problem in communication is the illusion that it has taken place.

— GEORGE BERNARD SHAW

Miracle May

In 1863, Mabel Hubbard lost her hearing from scarlet fever. She was five years old. A hearing specialist told her father, Gardiner Hubbard, that she would lose her speech in three months and that if she tried to talk, her voice would sound like "a steam locomotive." (Clearly, this guy needed some people skills!)

Hubbard and his wife, Gertrude, ignored the specialists. They wanted to help her maintain communication with the outside world. They began speaking to her directly at her eye line. May had a breakthrough when her mother showed her a picture of performer Mrs. Tom Thumb, from Barnum's Circus. Remembering her visit to the circus, May uttered the words, "Little lady." Her parents were ecstatic!

Dr. Howe, a visionary in education who was the head of Perkins Institute for the Blind, encouraged them even further. He had met hearing impaired students in Germany who could speak and read lips! There were no schools for the deaf in the U.S. at the time. With no curriculum or training, by trial and error (and the help of governess, Mary True), the Gardiners began to teach May lip reading. They understood that the quality of her future hinged on her ability to communicate.

A young elocution professor named Alec took May on as a student when she was fifteen. He had helped his father to develop visible speech, a system of symbols that helped that showed his students how to use their lips, tongues, palates, and teeth, to form sounds. Alec was working miracles in the deaf community, but he was doubtful that anyone could actually read lips… until he met May. Not only did May prove him wrong, but she also stole his heart.

Alec told May that her voice was naturally sweet. Unlike so many others, May was able to read Alec's lips easily and understand his instruction. She could tell that he truly cared about her. A world of communication opened up between them. He understood her completely. Three years later, with her parent's blessing, Alec married her. On July 11, 1877, Mabel Hubbard became Mrs. Alexander (Alec) Graham Bell.[1] The girl who was told she would never be able to communicate was being heard by one of the greatest minds in communication of all time.

Essential # 5: Effective Communication

Effective communication is the essential that is most needed in the workplace. In order to thrive, to grow, and to build out your dream, you have to be able to communicate. You want to be able to share your ideas, your hopes, and your struggles with your colleagues. In the workplace, effective communication and trust are the basis of relationship building. Like May, the quality of your future hinges on your ability to listen and be understood. (Unfortunately, you don't have Alexander Graham Bell to help you communicate more clearly!)

You may think that your ability to communicate depends solely on being able to articulate your thoughts to those around you, but **the most important skill for you to practice in effective communication is the art of listening**. Listening holds the key to understanding the person you are trying to communicate with. Understanding unlocks the relationship of trust that effective communication is built upon. Once that trust is in place, even when communication is rocky, there is a willingness to stay in the conversation and figure things out together.

The art of conversation lies in listening.

— MALCOLM FORBES

The Art of Listening

According to research, the average person hears up to 300,000 words per day...but only remembers 17%-25% of what they hear.[2] This seems about right. Have you ever left a conversation and thought, "I can't remember a single thing that person said!" It could be because you haven't honed your listening skills enough.

I used to tune out in meetings where the conversation didn't really affect me. I was bored by the things being said. So, I didn't listen. I forgot to engage in essential #2 – curiosity. The key to listening is getting curious. A conversation is an opportunity to learn something new, gain insight, and build trust.

Whoever is talking to you, whether it is a manager, a client, or a colleague, they are sharing part of their story with you. You may not be able to remember facts... but who can forget a good story? When you get curious about the people you are talking to, you get in on their story. That's when listening becomes powerful!

. . .

Get Curious… Get Listening

There are four different ways you can build out your listening skills.

1. Reading Body Language
2. Engage with Empathy
3. Ask Meaningful Questions
4. Build Understanding

Reading Body Language

Imagine that you are reading a story. At the beginning of the story, the character is described as having a giant grin, head thrown back to look at the sun, arms swinging wide as they stroll down the street. Just by these descriptions you know how this person feels. Joyful. Energetic. Excited. You know that, because since you were a tiny child you have been studying body language and reading social-emotional cues.

The New York Times reported that, "Albert Mehrabian, a pioneer researcher of body language in the 1950's, found that the total impact of a message is about 7 percent verbal (words only) and 38 percent vocal (including tone of voice, inflection, and other sounds) and 55 percent nonverbal."[3] That means that 93% of communication has nothing to do with actual words! Crazy, right? You can determine how someone is feeling without them saying a word.

Have you ever walked into a team meeting and you know what is going on... before you know what is going on? That is because you are read the room... the expressions and the postures of the people around the table: bored, prepared, tense, upbeat. It's all there, written on the faces of your co-workers.

Imagine someone at the table, sending these non-verbal cues:

1. Crossed arms
2. Furrowed brow
3. Tapping feet

How does this person feel? What signals are they sending? Closed off. Worried. Anxious.

Now consider a person displaying these non-verbal cues:

1. Smiling
2. Arm stretched out to greet a co-worker
3. Feet planted firmly

What message is this person sending? They feel happy. Welcoming. Confident.

It is amazing what you can "hear" someone saying to you, even when they don't speak to you. You can start to unravel their emotions and intentions by their posture and the looks on their faces. (Note: this is why so much can be lost in translation with e-mail or texting.) Communication is about way more than words. Being able to read body language helps you get the full message the person across the table from you is sending. Being able to read how someone is feeling is the gateway to empathy and understanding.

What you do speaks so loud that I cannot hear what you say.

— RALPH WALDO EMERSON

Engage with Empathy

Every story has a point of view. Point of view is crucial in communication. Take May and Alexander's story. May Hubbard's point of view was very different than her husband's. But Alexander was empathetic to May's struggle... not just because he worked with the hearing impaired, but because his own mother struggled with hearing loss. His mother's story impacted his own. One of the reasons why his relationship with May was so powerful was because Alexander engaged with empathy.

When you are listening to someone, you have the opportunity to see things from their point of view. You can step into their shoes, seeing the conversation from their side. This is called being "empathetic." When you understand the emotion or motivation behind their story, it helps you understand the choices they make, the way that they engage with others, and their reactions. Empathy enables you to make decisions and help others in light of their story. One of the best ways to grow empathy is to ask questions.

Empathy: The feeling that you understand and share another person's experiences and emotions; the ability to share someone else's feelings

---

Ask Questions

As a person, who has made his living asking questions, I have found it to be foundational in trust-building. Sales is less about selling someone on an idea and more about meeting a felt need. I can't help a client, if I don't know what they value, what their needs are, or how they want me to help them. When I am genuinely curious about who they are and what their needs are, they begin to trust me. (What I do with their answers to my questions determines how much they will continue to trust me.)

Imagine that one of your co-workers came into work super cranky. (You may already have one in mind!) He/she is short with you and turns their back to you in their cubicle. (Strong body language!) You are probably thinking, "What a jerk! I'm not talking to them!" (Zero communication!) Now, take a step back. Take a deep breath. And ask this person:

1. **How are you doing?** (This is a great question!

Remember, you want to hear their story and be empathetic. Get curious.)

2. **How can I help you?** (This is also a great question. There are no accusations here, just an affirmation that you are a team player and want to support your co-worker, client, or manager.)

It is easier to judge the mind of a man by his questions rather than his answers.

— PIERRE MARC-GASTON, DUC DE LEVIS

By asking these questions, you may find out that your co-worker has insomnia or that their good friend has cancer or that they are feeling overwhelmed by their workload. Any of these answers broadens your understanding of their situation, triggering empathy.

You may notice a shift in their demeanor when you take time to ask questions. Why? Because by asking, you show that you care! Caring builds trust. **Trust is the foundation of effective communication.** Voila! There is probably a shift in your perception of that person. This comes from stepping into their shoes and embracing empathy.

> When the trust account is high, communication is easy, instant, and effective.
>
> — STEPHEN R. COVEY

Now let's flip this example on its head. **What if you are the person who is feeling sleepless or sad or overwhelmed by work? How does it make you feel when someone takes the time to hear your story?** When someone cares about your wellbeing (and not just the project you are working on), you are more motivated to connect with them. Listening and empathy bring about a cycle of goodness.

When we hear each other's stories, understand each other's emotions, and encourage each other, it changes the atmosphere in the room. Empathy ushers in a sense of respect and mutual understanding. There is another way that understanding can be increased by communicating... by knowing each other's personality traits.

> Seek first to understand, then to be understood.
>
> — STEPHEN COVEY

Building Understanding

Building understanding is another key component of effective communication. Once you have gained insight about the person you want to communicate with, you have opened up an avenue of trust. This trust can be grown further when you understand people's personality profile.

When I began understanding how DISC impacted my own communication style, I realized how important it was to grow that platform of understanding with others. Success not only comes through being authentic (essential #1!) and understanding myself but also through understanding the behavioral profile of the people I work with. Knowing different communication styles helps me communicate in the best way I can, to get the most favorable result. The same can be true for you.

Let's go back and look at May and Alexander again.

1. Alexander wanted to help May communicate in the best way she could.
2. He engaged with empathy.
3. He asked questions in order to best help her.
4. Knowing her communication needs, he spoke clearly and annunciated so she could understand him. He was able to speak her "communication language."

What Is A Communication Style?

I love to talk to people. My preference is to meet someone face to face or have a phone conversation. I enjoy the interplay and bouncing thoughts and ideas off people. I am also able to read people much better when I can see their faces or hear their voices. I tend to process my thoughts and ideas verbally. This would be my communication style.

You might have a different preferred way to communicate. Maybe you like to think about what you are going to say when you interact with someone. Writing out your thoughts in an e-mail or text enables you to think through a process. Or maybe you like a couple of days to ruminate on an idea and get back to the person you are collaborating with. Often, our communication style is directly linked to our personality profile. Cool, right?

If I know that one of my clients likes phone conversations, I phone them. If they want to communicate by e-mail, I send e-mails. A great way to build trust and understanding is to connect with them in the way they best understand.

The best way to figure out someone else's communication language…is to ask them! Crazy, I know! (Here I go asking questions again!) When you are working with a co-worker or client, you can ask them their preferred method of communication. You can also ask them if they like communications to be short and concise or if they prefer detail. Asking these questions is yet another way to build understanding and show that you care.

At times, we may not get the opportunity to ask a person a direct question, and we still need to be able to diagnose their natural communication style. The best-communicated message is only effective if received. When our message is received, that is when we find success.

(For further professional development, The Stop Clowning Around Institute offers a course called "Connect 4 Communication." It is based on the DISC Behavioral Assessment and focuses on helping students become aware of their natural communication style. But more importantly, it helps them read the style of others so they can structure the communication to be received best by their audience.)

What's the Message?

When Alexander Graham Bell was growing up, he had a front-row seat to one of the best communicators at that time, his father. Alexander's mother had suffered hearing loss and had to use an ear trumpet to hear what they were saying. But Alexander's father didn't use the ear trumpet. He simply placed his lips against his wife's forehead and spoke to her. She could tell what he was saying by the subtle pressure against her forehead. His father's communication always came through loud and clear.[4]

It must have been an amazing experience for Alexander to see his mother so cherished and cared for by his father. That care and concern overflowed into his own life's work as a teacher and his care of his wife, May. Alexander's message to May also came through loud and clear. She was a valued, treasured partner in his life's work.

My life is my message.

— MAHATMA GHANDI

Sound Messaging

Getting your message across is the last step to effective communication. When you have opened the avenues of trust and understanding, you want to make sure that your message is easily understood. How you present yourself, your attitude, and your actions set the stage for sharing your message. Try the methods below to build sound messaging into your communication skills.

1. Use your understanding of body language to make a good impression. Keep your head up, smile, and offer a firm handshake. This is a way to convey confidence, and your confidence invites respect.
2. Be kind. People will want to hear from you and be influenced by you when you are kind. You want your character to back up your message. (When was the last time you wanted to listen to a jerk? Never, right?) Your kindness sets the stage for your message to be heard and accepted.
3. Be clear. The times that I have been unclear with my message are the times that miscommunication took place. Determine what information you want to share and what questions you want to ask before you

have a meeting or a call. This will make the
conversation easier for both of you.

4. Be patient. If you can tell that your message is not
coming across clearly, take time with your manager,
client, or colleague, to ensure that they understand
either what you are asking of them or the vital
information that you are relaying to them. Your
patience is another way that you show them that you
value them. (Another trust builder!)

Communication is a skill that you learn. It's like riding
a bicycle or typing. If you're willing to work at it, you
can rapidly improve the quality of every part of your
life.

— BRIAN TRACY

Know that what you have to say has value. You are learning
and growing more every day. As you begin working on
communicating effectively, know that it will take some
practice. The great thing is you will have lots of
opportunities every day to get better at it! Know that when
you care about others, building understanding and trust,
they will be more likely to do the same with you.

Practice Effective Communication

Here are some practical ways to incorporate effective communication into your day:

1. Make listening your favorite activity, and try a "talking fast." http://www.wellnessuprising.com/blog/2014/6/29/the-power-of-no-words-talk-fasting.

2. Take a course on communication and learn your natural communication style and how to identify the style of the message receiver. (http://stopclowningaround.com/connect4communication).

3. Make a game/challenge of social situations. Ask yourself how many interesting things you can learn about others during this event, meeting, or conversation?

4. Mentally prepare for communication in advance when possible. Think through potential connection ice breakers, things you would like to learn more about, and generate well-thought-out questions in advance, so you are more effective and not just thinking on your feet.

5. Develop a love and appreciation for humanity and recognize that all humans have value to offer. It's your job to find it and encourage it.

6. Embrace curiosity in listening. Enjoy learning new things about the people you talk to. Remember that everyone has a story to tell.

7. Put yourself in communication settings as an observer only. Try to shadow meetings of your boss, co-workers, and family. Don't engage, just observe

and learn from the best practices and failures of those you are observing. When you are not trying to figure out what to say next, you get a much greater context of the entire conversation and what is trying to be said.

Stop clowning around and utilize effective communication!

ESSENTIAL #6: FOCUSED ORGANIZATION

Organizing is what you do before you do something,

so that when you do it, it is not all mixed up.

— A.A. MILNE

Getting the Job Done

When I was a kid, I had a lot of chores. It was one of the ways that my parents taught me how to be responsible. I didn't love chores, especially chores that took place in the hot sun. One of my chores was picking potatoes in our garden. I had to bend over and dig down in the soil with a small shovel. Not the most fun, for sure. One afternoon while I was bored and tired of digging up endless potatoes, I noticed that three of the potatoes were very round. They were exactly the right size for juggling. Juggling is way more fun than picking potatoes!

Having watched a clown video demonstrating juggling using scarves, I was mesmerized by the process. I loved how easily the jugglers seemed to keep all the scarves in motion. I picked up the three potatoes and held them in my hands, feeling their weight and size. I didn't have any scarves, but I knew how I was going to spend my chore time. I started practicing. I dropped a lot of potatoes that afternoon, but I practiced over and over.

The trick to juggling is to put the same ball... in the same place... each time it comes around, so that the timing is right. There is an easy transition of moving ball to spot. The rhythm of it took a while to master, but I finally got it. I don't remember finishing potato picking that day, but something bigger had happened. I was a juggler!

Juggler for Life

I carried my sweet juggling skills with me into the workplace as a young professional. The buzz word at the time was "multi-tasking." **Multitasking is the attempt to handle all the tasks that you have at the same time, with the same level of attention, without dropping a single "ball."** If you can juggle your workload, your client issues, meetings with your manager, and still be home in time to play with your kids? You are an amazing multitasker!!!

When people multi-task, they often do multiple things badly.

— DR. DAVID SANBONMATSU, PSYCHOLOGY
PROFESSOR UNIVERSITY OF UTAH

Remember that the key to juggling is keeping all the balls (or potatoes) in the air, using the same rhythmic timing. **The problem with juggling tasks (not potatoes), is that there is no such thing as rhythmic timing in real life.** One task always ends up taking more time than others. All tasks are not equal. Some have more importance than others. In my multi-tasking endeavors, I always ended up dropping the ball.

Essential #6: Focused Organization

Life is messy. Work-life included. At work, do you feel like you are being asked to juggle 113 balls in the air at all times? Keeping one ball in the air is easy. Two is doable but more difficult. Add a third, and the struggle is real. The more tasks and priorities that are added, the more difficult it gets to manage your workload. And the crazy thing is? Other people keep throwing more tasks, jobs, events, and work your way (usually the ones they don't want to handle!) The more tasks you are juggling… the more balls you are dropping.

Like Dr. Sobanmatsu says… you are probably doing multiple things badly. I know I was. This is disheartening for someone who is working so hard, isn't it? Your struggle isn't because of a lack of effort but instead has to do with the reality of your complex brain function.

Your Beautiful Brain… Again

The American Association for the Advancement of Science says that the brain can only handle two complex tasks at a time. Neuroscientist Etienne Koechlin explains it this way, **"In terms of everyday behavior, you can cook and talk on the phone at the same time. The problem arises when you pursue three goals at the same time. Your prefrontal cortex will always discard one."**[1] (Your brain automatically drops the ball for you!)

This has to do with the way that tasks are distributed in the hemispheres of the brain. There is some conflicting research that does say that the brain can maybe also take on one more task, as long as it is something that doesn't interfere with the centers that are already being used, like eating. So, in other words, in your very best multi-tasking moment, you can e-mail, talk on the phone…and maybe eat a cookie at the same time. But at that point you'll have maxed out your brain's capacity to take on tasks.

Multi-tasking, as we've all heard it described, is a myth. You're not actually simultaneously handling tasks; your brain is just switching back and forth between the multiple goals you are trying to achieve. **Trying to manage multiple tasks at once is called cognitive switching or task-switching.**[2] Some crazy things happen when you switch things up on yourself like that.

1. You tend to make more mistakes.
2. It takes more time to complete tasks than if you just focused on one task at a time.
3. In a full day of switching back and forth between tasks, you can lose up to 40% of your productivity!

That's just sad. It is time to let go of your juggling mentality and lean into the essential of focused organization. Focused organization, once you figure out how to incorporate it into your life, can alleviate a whole lot of stress. And who doesn't want that?

Focus, people!

Focused organization starts by concentrating on one task at a time. When you lose the multi-tasking mindset, you let your brain function in the best possible way. You also organize your priorities in a way that can maximize your time and increase your productivity. Instead of trying to complete multiple tasks at once, just **take it one task at a time.**

So why is it so hard to focus? Lack of focus seems to be an issue across the board. With so much stimuli and so many distractions in the workplace (and at home!), it can be difficult to focus on anything. But when you decide to stop task-switching and give your most important task all of your attention, it allows you to be present in the moment. Instead of feeling scattered and rushed, you can push eliminate distractions and see true success.

Realize deeply that the present moment is all you ever have. Make the Now the primary focus of your life.

— ECKHART TOLLE

The One Thing

Back in the early 2000's, Gary Keller had a booming real estate business. He was the co-founder of Keller-Williams Realty, but he had bigger goals that he wanted to accomplish. He wanted to attract the best realtors in the industry to his business. He found he was able to do this when he and his team decided to get creative and narrow their focus. In an interview with *Forbes*, Gary Keller, author of *The One Thing* says, "You simply ask yourself in any given area of your life, **"What's the one thing I can do, such that by doing it everything else is easier or unnecessary?" That's it."**[3]

Keller used this principle with his own company when he wrote the book, *The Millionaire Real Estate Agent.* Writing a book about being the best person you could be in the real estate market changed the industry's perception of their company. The book is still a best-seller more than fifteen years after its release. Keller's focus on his goal established him as an expert in his field. He continues to write inspirational, challenging best-sellers that impact his field. Keller seems to know a little something about the power of focusing his energy on his topmost priority.

The key is not to prioritize what's on your schedule but to schedule your priorities.

— STEPHEN COVEY

Priorities. Priorities. Priorities.

The real question is... do you know what your priorities are? For today? This week? This month? This year? And more importantly, what is your top priority? This priority should get the most of your focus. **Complete that task to the best of your ability. And then move on to the next priority at hand.** When you give your number one priority most of your attention, you allow yourself to be all in, to lend all of your creativity, passion, and determination to that task, enabling you to actually complete it!

Keller's book, *One Thing: The Surprisingly Simple Truth Behind Extraordinary Results,* influenced the way that I prioritize and plan out my goals for the year with an ultimate five-year goal in mind. I ask myself, **what is the one thing I want to accomplish this year?** What is the one thing I want to achieve by the middle of this year? What is the one thing I want to achieve this month? This framework helps me plan backward. If the tasks that I am focusing on each day (even if they are good things) are not working towards accomplishing my goals, I find ways to eliminate them.

You've probably heard the sayings, "Time is of the essence" and "We're living on borrowed time." Time is a precious commodity. You never seem to have enough of it. You only get what you are given. You have to eliminate distractions through focused effort. Are the tasks you are spending the most time on focused on your top priority? Or do the menial least important tasks seem to take up most of your time?

It is not a daily increase but a daily decrease. Hack away at the inessentials.

— BRUCE LEE

Spend a moment thinking about your priorities. Answer the questions below:

What is the one thing I want to accomplish this year?

What is the one thing I want to accomplish by the middle of this year?

What is the one thing I want to accomplish this month?

What is the one thing I want to accomplish this week?

What do I spend the most time doing each day? Is this task (or tasks) helping me accomplish my goals? Why or why not?

Is there a time sucker that I need to eliminate in my daily routine so that I can focus on my number one priority? If so, what is it?

Break your year-end goal down into necessary landmark goals. Determine what appropriate tasks you need to achieve for your day, week, month, and half-yearly goals to move you towards that year-end goal. If you have tasks that don't align with your goals, get rid of them!

Things which matter most must never be at the mercy of things which matter least.

— GOETHE

Work/Life Balance

If multi-tasking was the buzzword when I started my career, work/life balance is the buzzword now. That is because a lot of us have all the work... and no life! Like I stated in the paragraph above, giving your attention to your most important priority will help relieve stress. One of the reasons is that it enables you to sort out your priorities. One of the most important priorities should be your family and home life. This will bring that balance you are looking for.

If I were to ask you what is, hands down, the most important thing in thing in your life, you would probably say your family. So would I. Yet in a 2018 study of 2000 families across the United States, **the average quality time spent together was 37 minutes per day.**[4] (Okay... that's is just depressing.) That is 2.5% of your day. What is happening with the other 97.5% of your day? Where is that balance you are looking for?

If your top priority is your family, how is it that you are spending so little time on that priority? Probably because you are working like crazy so they can eat, have a roof over their heads, and have clothes! This is where time blocking comes in. Time blocking isn't a new idea, but maybe it is a new way for you to think about re-organizing not just your workday, but your family life.

I separate my goals into time blocks – work time blocks and family time blocks. I work to achieve my business goals during business hours and my family goals during family hours.

My workday starts before the rising of the sun.

- **I have three main priorities** that I want to get done each day, and I break those priorities into smaller tasks. Of the three priorities, the one that is most important? Gets most of my time. (See how I did that?)
- **I block out my day with flexibility,** knowing that some tasks will require more of my attention. This creates a guideline and expectation of what my day will look like.
- **I eliminate distractions and focus on my top priority.** (More on those pesky distractions below.)

My workday ends at 5:30 p.m.

- **I set aside a half hour to connect with my wife** and talk as we start our evening together.
- **I set aside around two and a half hours each night with my kids.**
- **Weekends are set aside for family.**

These are general blocks that give my family the priority it deserves, but I am always flexible. Sometimes I have work trips. Sometimes family requires more time. I adjust with the days, knowing that both my work and family will get my full attention. I want to have a decent margin in my life, with both work and family so that I have time to rest my body and mind and replenish my energy.

. . .

Pomodoro Method

Research points out that the human mind is not meant to focus on a single task for long periods.[5] Many productivity experts utilize the Pomodoro Method. It is a practice of focusing on a singular task for twenty-five minutes at a time with a five-minute break. They set their alarm to ensure they make use of each valuable minute. Many swear by this method because it allows them to focus on a task and not deal with FOMO (Fear of Missing Out) on another important task.[6]

In addition, when they give a specific timeframe for the task, the brain kicks into overdrive working to ensure the task gets done in time. The other bonus is that the frequent breaks allow you to step away from the desk for a quick walk or some other kind of movement. This action break reduces the physical stress and resulting anxiety that can build up throughout the day.[7] This stress-reduction enhances one's ability to focus on productivity once work begins.[8]

Distraction Hacks

I love the scene in the Disney movie, *Up,* where Dug the Dog meets the main characters, Russell and Carl. Dug is mid-sentence, explaining his purpose in life (his master made him a collar so he could talk), when he yells out, "Squirrel!" He can't help but surrender to his distractions… it is a squirrel, after all!

Dug's response is a great metaphor for work life. Here you are, dialed in on your life's purpose, focused and organized, and all of a sudden, you yell out, "Phone!" (It is a phone after all!) It really has never been easier to be distracted!

To keep myself focused, I have put some distraction hacks in place in my work and family life.

1. I don't try to achieve business goals during family hours and vice versa.
2. I don't take phone calls from unknown numbers. I let them leave a message and then get back to them.
3. I don't look at emails on my phone, and when I do check them at specific intervals. Most e-mails don't have to be dealt with immediately. My first e-mail check is at 11 a.m. I find a bad e-mail can ruin the start of my day.
4. I let my clients and colleagues know my personal boundaries. They know when they can get ahold of me. I always respond in a timely manner, so they don't worry if they don't hear back from me immediately. (Remember, we are the ones who put pressure on ourselves to be available 24/7! Give yourself margin.)
5. I don't engage in social media during work hours unless it is required by my job. If you decide to engage in social media at the office or at home, use an app to limit your time. As a professional, it is best to be a content creator, not a content consumer.

There is no worse feeling at the end of the day than feeling like you worked hard, but didn't accomplish anything substantial. What are the things that distract you? Work methodically to weed out distractions and keep persevering.

List the top three things that distract you, along with the distraction hack you are going to employ to keep yourself organized and focused.

Try not to do too many things at once.

Know what you want, the number one thing today and tomorrow.

Persevere and get it done.

— GEORGE ALLEN

Like all of the other essentials you are learning about, leaning into focused organization takes practice. As you work towards focusing on your goals, ordering your priorities, stripping down the inessentials, and weeding out distractions, you will find that no two days look alike. Focused organization isn't perfection. It is a framework to lay out your days so that you can accomplish all you can as you are becoming the person you are meant to be.

Practice Focused Organization:

- Create a daily task list. At the end of the day, move unfinished events to the next day. The thought of having to move them will provide motivation to complete them on the assigned day.
- Create a priority list of your top three priorities that are from the daily task list. Complete these tasks first.
- Block out time on your calendar. Tell yourself when and what you will be working on throughout the day. Be the boss of your schedule.
- Use distraction blocker apps to help you manage your distractions on the phone and computer.
- Journal your use of time for a week. Analyze how you are spending time and learn what can/must go from those habits.
- Hire a coach or seek help from a supervisor to hold you accountable. (Friends may not hold you accountable to your desired standard, because they don't want to offend you. Coaches and supervisors will!)

Stop clowning around and lean into focused organization!

ESSENTIAL #7: COHESIVE COLLABORATION

No one can whistle a symphony. It takes a whole orchestra to play it.

— H.E. LUCCOCK

The Unicycle Approach

I have early memories of a circus clown riding a one-wheeled bike. The lone spotlight followed him, highlighting his amazing tricks. He was quick, nimble, and showy. He circled back and forth, weaving in and around the ring, seemingly defying logic. He was the perfect picture of wild color, control, and balance. He made it look easy. I couldn't take my eyes off him. He was the star of the show as far as I was concerned.

Fast forward twenty years, when my young next-door neighbor offered to teach me how to ride a unicycle. I knew how to ride a bike. How hard could it be to ride a unicycle? Apparently, pretty hard. Even just getting on proved treacherous. (Have you ever been catapulted from something with a single wheel? It's terrifying!) Although I tried for weeks, I could never master the art of riding this one-wheeled wonder. It mastered me.

The funny thing is, early in my career, riding solo was my go-to. I was all about me and what gains I could make to get to the top on my own. This mindset was a throw-back to my school days. I hated group projects.

- It always seemed like one or two people did all the work.
- You didn't get to choose your own team.
- There weren't enough varied skill sets in the group.
- There were too many different opinions about how to go about the project.

Group work was a big bummer. I would much rather have knocked out the project on my own time, using my own expertise, in my own way.

I felt the same way about team projects in the workplace.

- Working together just seemed to breed conflict.

- Collaboration was messy. (Too many fingers in the pie.)
- Too many viewpoints made reaching the end goal difficult.
- It was easier to just do things by myself.

When I closed a deal or came up with a new strategy, I was the star of the show. My own show. (With my own proven capabilities...and weaknesses) I wanted to be the best in my job and my industry. Going it alone seemed the best route.

Coming together is a beginning. Keeping together is progress. Working together is success.

— HENRY FORD

The Unicycle Approach is something I mastered... my ideas, my skills, my goals, my way. It was definitely more of a self-centered approach to work. One that worked for me... for a while. The problem was that in my attempts to be the best, I always came up short. There was always someone who was better than me. Someone who closed more sales and made more deals. Someone who had more influence and got promoted quicker than I did. I have always been pretty competitive. My competitive lone wolf approach left me feeling empty and negative about my own abilities. Working on my own wasn't all it was cracked up to be. I needed some cohesive collaboration in my life.

. . .

Essential #7: Cohesive Collaboration

Our seventh essential, cohesive collaboration, unleashes the power of team dynamics. Working on your own, promoting yourself, and trying to achieve great results consistently can prove to be exhausting and discouraging. You may have some amazing strengths in the field you are working in, but it is highly likely that you also have some amazing weaknesses. While you may think it is easier to work on your own, easier isn't always better. To become the you that you are meant to be, you need the power of a great team with you, behind you, and rooting for you. Your success depends on it.

Collaboration With A Capital "C"

In 2000, when Steve Jobs relocated Pixar, he had a vision for collaboration. Instead of using three different buildings, he placed the entire company in one building with a common area in the center. He knew that in order for the company to grow and succeed, collaboration had to be celebrated. Pixar needed to be a collective of artistry and technology. Artists and techies tend to see things differently. They come at problems with different mindsets and methods. They may share the same goals, but they have completely different processes. Jobs envisioned a marriage of the two.

None of us is as smart as all of us.

— KEN BLANCHARD

The atrium at the center of the building served as a melting pot of ideas and inspiration. The mailboxes, cafeteria, gift shop, and meeting rooms were all found at the building's center, in natural gathering places where people could interact and brainstorm. The results were stunning. Pixar could easily be seen as one of the most collaborative companies in the world. Steve Jobs knew how powerful collaboration could be. Inviting the best minds in the tech and art industries to work together changed the movie industry forever.

Bring Your Best

Steve Jobs intuited what I did not. Collaboration, not competition, is what sets you up for success. I misunderstood the power of teams and cooperation... basing it on my disappointing childhood experiences. I didn't have to be the best, but if I brought my best, and the rest of my team brought their best, our collaboration could unleash success.

Forbes reported on a Stanford study of collaboration, stating that "Participants in the research who were primed to act collaboratively stuck at their task 64% longer than their solitary peers, whilst also reporting higher engagement levels, lower fatigue levels and a higher success rate."[1] It seems like a no brainer that sharing a project's workload would be helpful, but to know that those who collaborate are capable of achieving more? Sign me up!

Collaboration has another great byproduct – happiness! (Who doesn't want to be happier? I do!) Atlassian, a software company with a focus on collaborative tools, surveyed over 1,000 team members and found "that when honest feedback, mutual respect, and personal openness were encouraged, team members were 80 percent more likely to report higher emotional well-being."[2] When we work well together, there is a sense of accomplishment, as well as a sense of joy.

Competition in the workplace can be divisive, but collaboration tends to motivate and energize co-workers. As you are growing in collaboration skillset, you will soon find out (like I did) that your responsibilities, your workload, and your lack of available time can overwhelm you. Collaborating with a team or colleague is the only way to grow beyond your initial start. **There can be a cultural shift (this starts with you) of not being the best, but bringing your best.**

When you bring your best, you are measuring your own ability, not comparing yourself to others. You are able to control your own growth and ability ... not anyone else's. Everyone has different starts and struggles in life. Comparing and competing in the workplace rarely leads to a positive outcome. But when you start competing against yourself and collaborating with others, it is a powerful shift.

You can continue to grow, learn, and improve throughout your career, while partnering with others doing the same. The result is success, not just for one, but for all involved. That is powerful!

The strength of the team is each individual member.

The strength of each member is the team.

— PHIL JACKSON

Fire Power

In Shawn Achor's book, *Big Potential*, he shares a powerful illustration of collaboration. In the year 1935, biologist Dr. Hugh Smith witnessed a natural phenomenon that shifted his views on nature bringing order out of chaos. While visiting a mangrove forest in Southern Asia, the forest lit up like a lightning storm ... but from within. It did this not once, but multiple times. What he discovered was that a critical mass of lightning bugs were working together to light up the forest.

It was later proven that the massive light show was a highly charged, highly attractive mating call! When the male lightning bugs lit up simultaneously, they experienced a 79% higher response rate by the female population. (That gives new meaning to the term "wingman"!) Achor goes on to say, "Like the lightning bugs, once we learn to coordinate and collaborate with those around us, we all begin to shine brighter, both individually and as an ecosystem."[3] There is power in working together. Anyone who has ever had the pleasure of working with a good team can attest to that.

The power of collaboration translates just as well in the business realm. In an enlightening podcast, I interviewed Sara Mays, former VP of Asset Protection for Barnes and Noble. She recently launched her own company, coaching others in growing their own retail business. Sara said, "Growing a business requires utilizing the strengths of those around you and celebrating their accomplishments. Your team may be employees or vendors or a combination of both, but collaborating with them to identify opportunities will move a business forward.

I've always been a big believer in seeking ideas from the end-user. I recently was working with a client to grow his practice in a secondary location. We asked his staff for ideas, and they came up with several which they immediately implemented. Within fourteen days, the numbers had improved by more than 50%. Ideas included focusing on the convenience of the secondary location by geographical area and working with the vendor to update the website to highlight this fact. And to top it off, the person that came up with the key part of the geographical idea was the newest staff member."

Collaboration strengthens companies. It strengthens teams. And it strengthens you individually because the power of your company and team enables you to become the person you were meant to be.

Strengths and Weaknesses

Take a moment and write down your top three strengths and weaknesses. Think about how you incorporate these traits into your workday.

STRENGTHS

1.
2.
3.

WEAKNESSES

1.
2.
3.

Now brainstorm the people on your team who are strong in the areas that you are weak. Write their names next to your weakness. Now, think about how you can utilize their strengths and collaborate with them. Are there ways that you could build up their weaknesses with your strengths? Is there a way that you can work together to enjoy greater success as a team than you would individually?

The Power Of We vs. Me

It took me a while to realize that it makes a whole lot of sense for me to work within my strengths and align myself with people who have opposite strengths than I do. Most people tend to gravitate towards people like themselves. You often find that within a company, managers tend to hire people like themselves. But we need people who are different than we are. Diversity is necessary for us to achieve the success we long for. Colleagues and managers with different viewpoints, processes, and skill sets are an asset as you build out your career.

Martin Davidson, author of *The End of Diversity as We Know It*, says, "Organizations that truly leverage difference cultivate the capability to engage with and learn from diverse stakeholders, including employees, customers, partners, and communities. They use what they learn to explore how they can do the work of their organization more effectively."[4] Each person is needed, even those who view work and life differently than you do.

Imagine that your company is a finely tuned car. Each component of the car is working together to move this giant machine forward. You need all the different car components, the body, the engine, the chassis, the braking system, etc., for the car to function properly. None of these components work in the same way. None of them utilize the same instruments or tools to achieve success at what they do. This is common sense.

Now, if I told you, all you need to build a brand-new car is a pile of wheels, you would look at me like I had lost my mind.

You know that you need a whole lot more than tires to build a functional car. But often, you and I come into the workplace and gravitate to "a pile of wheels." We only want to work with people who have the same skill set and strengths that we do! We think that we can accomplish what we want without utilizing the other departments or working with those with different skill sets than we have. If you want to move forward, in your company, and your life, you need to seek out those who need your strengths and partner with those whose strengths build up your weaknesses.

While I can still work to improve my weaknesses, there is a much greater return on my effort when focusing on strengths and collaborating with others. I not only strive to collaborate with my team but with other departments. Like the different components of the automobile lending to its performance, we each bring different skills and gifts to our organization.

It is amazing what you can accomplish if you don't care who gets the credit.

— HARRY S. TRUMAN

As you begin to unleash cohesive collaboration in your life, take time to evaluate your DISC profile and the different profiles of those around you. This will help you identify those who you could be a help to and those whose skills you would benefit from. Find ways to work with those that you normally wouldn't. Remind yourself to be open to different viewpoints and processes than those you are used to. Ditch the unicycle approach! These mindful collaborations will stretch you and help you grow as you cross the skills gap and become the person you are meant to be!

Practicing Cohesive Collaboration:

- Take the DISC Assessment and understand your personality/behavioral style.
- Take a DISC course to fully understand your profile and the tendencies of those of other behavioral styles. The goal is to understand and appreciate the strengths of each profile.
- Build or put yourself on a diverse team of people with varying strengths and skills.
- Ask someone strong in an area that you are weak in to help you by taking a task that they excel at and return the value by taking one of their tasks that you excel at.

Stop clowning around and unleash cohesive collaboration!

ESSENTIAL #8: ENDURING FLEXIBILITY

The measure of intelligence is the ability to change.

— ALBERT EINSTEIN

Bookbinders and Balloons

In 1805, young Michael Faraday was an apprentice to a bookbinder. It was a good position for him since he was the son of a blacksmith and had little formal schooling. He had, however, learned to read and write in Sunday School. As a bookbinder's apprentice, he had the opportunity to read the books that he was binding. He took a special interest in the *Encyclopedia Britannica* and its insights about electricity. His curiosity got the better of him, and he began experimenting with electrochemistry in his spare time.[1]

A few years later, Faraday was able to attend a lecture by the great chemist, Sir Humphry Davy. He was mesmerized. Davy was on the cusp of changing the world's understanding of chemistry. In hopes of a career shift, Faraday bound his notes of Davy's lecture and sent them to the scientist...along with a request for employment. Davy didn't have a place open in his lab at the time but invited Faraday to join his work in 1812. This was Faraday's big pivot. The giant change that would launch his career and his life. Bookbinder to scientist. His life would never be the same. Neither would the world of science.

Pivot! Pivot! Pivot! Pivot! Pivot! Pivot!

— ROSS, *FRIENDS*

Having found his passion and life's work, Faraday went on to make one scientific discovery after and another. Learning from the master, he made foundational discoveries in metallurgy, electricity, and magnetism. But in 1824, when he was experimenting with helium and its buoyant properties, he came up with a different creation altogether.

In order to test the capabilities of the element, he needed a way to enclose it. By pressing the edges of two sheets of rubber together and powdering the interior with flour so it wouldn't stick, Faraday invented the modern-day helium balloon. The rubber that he used was tacky and resilient, making it the perfect medium to use.

More Thoughts On Balloons

Since that time, balloons have been used in party planning, medical procedures, and in experiments on the planet Venus. They are highly versatile in their use. Before Faraday's invention, balloons were made from animal bladders and intestines.[2] (There is a whole lot of wrong in that sentence right there.)

Within a year of his invention, balloon kits were being sold on the general market. However, the sausage-shaped balloons used for sculpturing weren't sold until the 1930's. Those balloons have a slightly different makeup, with added strength and flexibility.[3] (Keep that thought in mind!)

You may be wondering why I find balloon facts so interesting. First, any clown worth his red nose can craft a wiener dog out of a sculpturing balloon. (I felt an inordinate amount of pride the first time I twisted my first balloon sculpture.) And second, it is important to remember that as we talk about our eighth essential – enduring flexibility – a sculpturing balloon is the perfect metaphor for your flexible attitude in an ever-changing workplace environment.

Flexible: adaptable, adjustable, alterable, changeable, elastic, fluid, malleable, modifiable, pliable, variable

In 2017, a study conducted by the American Psychological Association found that almost 50% of all workers surveyed said they were affected in the past year, or were going to be affected in the upcoming, by changes in their organization. The workers experiencing change were twice as likely to experience stress than workers with a stable environment.[4]

While you may like to have a stable work environment, it is highly likely that some type of change will take place in your workplace within this upcoming year.

While some people love to change up their lives, DISC statistics show that nearly 70% of those profiled, fall in the Steadiness category.[5] Those with an S profile tend to struggle with adapting quickly to change or with unclear expectations. Stress affects each person differently.

An earlier study by the APA examined the symptoms of stress in the workplace. Researchers found that common physical and psychological symptoms of stress were fatigue, headaches, teeth grinding, muscle tension (massage, anyone?), irritability, nervousness, and feeling as though you could cry. (Just reading through the symptoms might be enough to make you cry!)

It is clear that both change and stress are alive and kicking in the workplace. They seem to be partnering up. This could have to do with how humans perceive stress – as a negative. Change is hard for most of us. We like our routines, certainty, and knowing that our jobs are stable. Organizational change unleashes uncertainty...and apparently, the need for mouth guards.

So, how can you guard against stress when change seems inevitable? Let's think back to essential #2 – curiosity and neuroplasticity. **What would happen if you changed the way that you looked at change?** What if you decided that change in your workplace was not a negative, but **an opportunity to be flexible, to shift your perspective, and a chance to pivot?**

Nothing is so painful to the human mind as a great and sudden change.

— MARY WOLLENCRAFT SHELLEY,
FRANKENSTEIN

Balloon Sculpturing and Brain Bending

Balloon sculpturing is gratifying work. I'll never forget twisting my first few balloons, first, a simple sword, next a dog, and then a French poodle. Not filling the balloons completely allowed me to make more intricate designs. Some of the most inventive designs required small, carefully planned pops. The calculated pops didn't break the balloon but gave it a more definitive shape. Some of my most

ESSENTIAL #8: ENDURING FLEXIBILITY | 185

elaborate designs involved multiple balloons and multiple pops. I practiced and practiced and the more confident I grew in my ability, the better the sculptures I created.

I thought I was pretty cool until I started watching Youtube videos. The creativity showcased there was amazing... and humbling. *Twisted,* a balloon sculpturing documentary, revealed that there are a whole lot of twisting people out there bringing smiles to the world with their craft.

I don't think you can use balloon sculpturing on your resume. I have never seen anyone promoted because of their ability to twist balloons. (I know I wasn't!) But **my most impressive colleagues and my best managers have succeeded in their careers because they knew how to "act like balloons."**

These flexible folks:

- are resilient (more on that with Essential #10)
- can shift direction multiple times allowing for multiple iterations of their careers
- permit change to help them become better than they were before
- leave room in their lives for margin and internal adjustment – they know that inflexibility leads to breakdowns
- know that they are stronger and have a broader reach when they team up with others

The ability to pivot or to take change in stride can define your career. Like a balloon taking a twist or pop, change creates new opportunities and can launch you in a new direction. It has to do with the direction you allow your thoughts to take when you experience change. How is your brain bent? Do you think (repeatedly... systemically) that all change is bad? Or do you allow your brain to dwell on the positive aspects of change?

To improve is to change. To be perfect is to change often.

— WINSTON CHURCHILL

Seeing Change Differently

Your ability to be flexible in tough situations helps you survive. You need to ask yourself, *how well can I adjust and adapt and continue* to *be great to myself?* I won't lie to you. A lot of times, change is hard. Sometimes change just sucks. But choosing to hate change... doesn't make it any easier.

You can learn to think of the discomfort of change as similar to the discomfort involved in exercise. You may not like how it makes you feel at that moment, but you can appreciate the benefits later. Flexibility is only brought about by practice. *Have you ever tried to touch your toes after sitting at your desk for eight hours straight? Sometimes you can't get past your shins. Becoming flexible takes* time. The same muscles that are tight and tense can grow limber over time. The more you stretch, the warmer your muscles get. You are able to accommodate a deeper stretch. Your confidence grows.

Psychology Today says that while our brains may be hardwired to resist change and uncertainty, they can also be trained to be malleable.[6] That is great news! You can re-train your brain to welcome change (and possibly even enjoy it!). As you are learning to think differently about change, you will want to make sure that you allow yourself the time and space you need to make the necessary adjustments.

Margin

Like I said earlier, change can be difficult and doesn't always feel great. But one of the ways you can bend your brain to think about change in a new way is to give yourself margin. Space. Room to breathe. Don't expect perfection from yourself in every new situation. I talked a little about margin with essential #7 - focused organization. **But times of workplace turbulence and change require even more margin in your life.** You may need to engage in some new practices as you experience the stress of a new situation.

You can give in to the stress and become irritable or angry about the changes taking place in your life. Or you can nurture yourself during this time.

Develop flexibility and you will be firm;

Cultivate yielding and you will be strong.

— LEIZI

Whenever you start a new balloon sculpture, you have to give yourself plenty of room for the twist, turns, and changes in the balloon. You never blow it up to full capacity. Adjustments will have to be made along the way. In the same way, think about your next steps when you are getting ready to accommodate a big change or shift in your life. Give yourself room to adjust and make mistakes.

Some ways to add margin into your life:

1. Be intentional about new activities you are taking on. Don't tackle multiple new interests at once.
2. If you know that your new work will be stressful, schedule time for rest and rejuvenation at the end of your day.
3. Set aside time for meditation where you calmly focus on a single thought at a time for clarity.
4. Take some time out to go for a walk during your workday.
5. Pay attention to the physical cues that your body is giving you. If you are tense, get up, move around and stretch.
6. If you are having anxious thoughts, tell yourself the truth. *This change is hard, but I am navigating it.* Focus

on the positive aspects of change in your mind.
Opportunity. Growth. New Challenges

7. Breathe. Literally. Take deep breaths. Change is a season. You will get through it.

Flexibility is the key to stability.

— JOHN WOODEN

As you develop your enduring flexibility and become more adaptable, you are actually literally becoming more stable. Once you recognize that change is inevitable and that you don't have to panic when it comes, you become more confident in the face of change. Although your boss may change, your company may be acquired, or your job description may shift, you learn to navigate changes without being derailed.

You can take constructive feedback and learn from it. You can weather a career change without crumbling. Being flexible in the face of change allows you to grow. Seeing change as a chance to pivot and branch out in your own career, can launch you in a new direction that you are passionate about. Learning how to nurture yourself when you are stressed out grounds you, no matter the situation that you are facing.

As you become flexible, you may notice that others experiencing change are drawn to you. Your emotional steadiness and your ability to thrive in a shifting environment will inspire and encourage those who are experiencing the same thing. **Even when it feels uncomfortable, act like a balloon.** Adjust. Twist. Give yourself space to breathe. You will be the stronger for it.

Change is inevitable. Growth is optional.

— JOHN MAXWELL

Practice Enduring Flexibility:

- Stretch yourself. Take small challenges that cause you minor anxiety and force yourself to act and overcome.
- Fail on purpose – Go for a drive in your city, take a new route (without GPS), allow yourself to get lost (fail). Recognize what was learned while you were lost.
- During a stressful situation, ask yourself, "What is the worst that can happen?" "If that happens, what will I do?" As you re-frame the situation in your mind. You will find that very little will hold you back.

Stop clowning around and engage in enduring flexibility!

ESSENTIAL #9: CREATIVE PROBLEM-SOLVING

Problems are nothing but wake-up calls for creativity.

— GERHARD GSCHWANDTNER

Creativity Wake-Up Call

In 1979, James Dyson realized he had a problem. He hated his vacuum cleaner. His strong feelings about vacuum cleaners had been established during childhood while doing chores with his mom. His mom's vacuum cleaner was frequently clogged with dust and debris. Changing the flimsy paper bag unleashed a cloud of dust into the air. The vacuum left fluff and particles behind on the floor because of poor suction. It bothered him that he had to pick up... after a product that was supposed to pick up. There were so many problems with this machine that was supposed to be a problem-solver.

We cannot solve our problems with the same thinking we used when we created them.

— ALBERT EINSTEIN

One day, while doing chores alongside his wife, Dierdre, Dyson had enough. He decided to solve the problem of the dusty, suctionless vacuum. He got creative. As a designer and engineer, he repurposed the technology that he had used to create an industrial cyclone tower for his company to creating cyclone technology for a vacuum cleaner. It took five years and over 5,000 prototypes, but he solved the problem. He created a new state-of-the-art bagless vacuum cleaner.[1] Forty years and three billion dollars later, James Dyson is still creating and still innovating.

Essential #9: Creative Problem-Solving

A question and answer are both found in essential #9 - creative problem-solving. What solves problems? Creativity. The need for innovation is ever-present in our world. Ever had a problem? Yep. Me, too. Ever experience a problem at work? Every day? Yep. Me, too. The problem with problems is that we see them as... problems. In reality, **problems are opportunities.** A real problem-solver is an innovator, an explorer, a conflict resolver, and a world helper. What could be better than that?

Problem-solving incorporates all of the previous essentials we have discussed: **audacious authenticity, emotional steadiness, avid curiosity, relational development, effective communication, focused organization, cohesive collaboration, and enduring flexibility.**

- Bring your authentic self to the problem-solving process. Your skillset and outlook will help solve the problem.
- Most problems are challenging. Emotional steadiness allows you to breathe and to think logically.
- Get curious and have a growth mindset while solving the problem.
- Draw on the wisdom of your support team. Utilize those relationships that you have cultivated.
- Be focused in your approach, giving the problem your full attention.
- Work with others and leverage their strengths in your areas of weakness.
- Last but not least, be flexible... things might not go as planned. You may not be able to solve the problem in a day (Dyson's 5000+ prototypes!).

Every essential that you have learned up until now sets the stage for you to be a creative problem-solver!

A problem is a chance for you to do your best.

— DUKE ELLINGTON

So Many Problems in the World, So Little Creativity

In 2016, Bloomberg surveyed 1,251 recruiters at 457 companies, asking them what attributes they looked for in new hires and specifically, the ones they had the most trouble finding.[2] Across the board, creative problem-solving ranked among the highest. The World Economic Forum listed complex problem-solving and creativity as their #1 skill and #3 skill (respectively) needed to thrive in the current technological age.[3] There is an urgent need for innovators in the workplace. Every industry, from business to medicine to education, needs people who are willing to take the time to sit with problems, get curious, and come up with inventive solutions.

Life is a crisis - so what!

— MALCOLM BRADBURY

Problem-solving isn't particularly easy, so it makes sense that it is not a skill that is easy to cultivate. People would like their problems to go away... without them actually addressing them. They are either too busy to spend time with the problem or don't see the value in wrestling or struggling with an issue. But problem-solving is nothing new in the human experience. It is introduced early on in the education process.

From figuring out how to structure a sentence to a child's first attempt at subtraction, children's minds are working to bring about solutions. Literary interventionist, Kate Mills, has an interesting method of helping her students work through their problems. She gives them a difficult math problem and instructs them, "Your job is to get yourselves stuck—or to allow yourselves to get stuck on this problem—and then work through it, being mindful of how you're getting yourselves unstuck."[4] No matter what field you are in, you have the same job as Mills' students.

If you are going to learn how to problem-solve creatively, you are going to want to get comfortable with the idea of "getting stuck and unstuck." Throughout the problem-solving process, there are multiple challenges and failures. But each attempt and failure can be seen as you getting one step closer to being unstuck.

My Big Problem

I was twenty-seven when I was hired into my first national accounts position at my company. I had succeeded as a local commercial rep, and they believed I could make it in the big leagues. I was excited, coming into the role. I had been promised some big-name accounts. There was a huge opportunity to work with large Fortune 500 companies. What my superiors didn't tell me was that our company had failed to serve these companies effectively in the past, and they were no longer doing business with us.

I was more than a little shocked when I made my first few phone calls only to hear that these amazing companies were not interested in meeting with me... let alone working with me. I was stuck. And I needed a way to get unstuck. I got creative. I thought about my new job in terms of my marriage. That might seem weird, but hear me out.

Early on in my career, Michelle and I had gone through a rocky period in our marriage, a time when Michelle was talking, and I wasn't particularly listening. I wasn't making her a priority. I had a whole lot going on. There was no margin, no work/life balance to be found. (I needed essential #6 bad!) I thought Michelle was the one with the problem and that she needed to get over herself. (Free marriage advice bonus: Don't ever, ever, ever let the words "get over yourself" come out of your mouth. It won't end well.)

Michelle got my attention when she told me I could either listen to what she had to say... or not be married to her anymore. Suddenly, I started listening. The shift in my attitude and my striving to understand her shifted the future of our relationship.

In approaching these Fortune 500 companies, I realized they needed to be listened to and understood. The problem wasn't that we couldn't accommodate their needs as a company. The problem was that trust had been broken, and my first job was to rebuild that trust. That started with listening. (Essential #5) I figured no one was listening to the customer and trying to understand the root problem. (More on this later in the chapter!)

With a few calls, I was finally able to get some facetime. Rather than trying to sell a product at these meetings, I simply asked questions about our customer history and where we had failed them. I asked them to identify what we could do better. Each company appreciated my care for their problem. In several cases, I went back and worked internally with our leadership, giving some options to work through the problems these dissatisfied customers were having.

Problems are only opportunities in work clothes.

— HENRY KAISER

In each scenario, I found my way back to the customer, gave a solution, and showed how the solution could be implemented in their company. I gave them more than a promise, I gave them a plan. A solution to their unique problem. In each case, the customer agreed to move forward with these solutions. They worked. I was shocked and thrilled when the orders started following behind.

Problems are not always bad, and you don't need to run from them or ignore them. When you are struggling to get unstuck, you don't need to blame someone else. Take responsibility for solving the problem. Even if you didn't create the problem, you may still be the perfect person to solve it. Face the conflict head-on. If you can help someone resolve an issue or sort through their mess, they can transform from a dissatisfied customer or a disgruntled supervisor to your biggest fan. (Who doesn't love having their problems solved?)

Problems are opportunities for growth and improvement, and they invite more loyalty from the person you are working with. All anyone (customers, employees, co-workers, managers) is looking for is respect, a listening ear, and someone willing to help. Once you help someone solve a problem, you build trust and make a fan. When you get unstuck, you help the people you are working with get unstuck, too. The upside to them getting unstuck is they want to keep you around.

Digging Down To The Root Of The Problem

Sometimes a truckload of small problems can mask the root of the main problem. Since our family moved into our latest house, we have continually had issues with landslides in the back yard. These are accompanied by mud and flooding. We have tried to shore up the landslides in multiple ways, by adding dirt to different areas, but to no avail.

Finally, I hired a geo-tech engineer. It was through his expertise that we found the root of the problem. The contractor who had built our house placed all the dirt he'd dug out for the basement on top of dead trees. At first, there wasn't a problem. Everything looked fine. But as the trees began to decompose, they created empty pockets of space beneath the dirt, causing it to cave in and slide. Adding more dirt only compounded the problem. According to the geo-tech, the whole area had to be excavated, re-filled, and compacted into a solid surface.

This process made me re-think how I attack a problem. I can spend a lot of time and money addressing surface issues, but the problem is not solved until I understand the root. Until the underlying issue is taken care of, nothing I do on the surface matters.

In the case of my Fortune 500 clients, it wasn't just that our company hadn't provided the best service, but that trust had been broken. Trust was the root issue. That had to be addressed before I could move forward and offer to provide service again.

If you are not sure how to get to the root of the problem and problem-solve creatively, I have a method you can put in place called S.T.O.P. It reminds you to stop and think before you take your first action steps!

. . .

S.T.O.P.

When you are facing a problem in the workplace or your career, you have the essentials in your back pocket to help you through the process. But S.T.O.P. can help unleash your problem-solving capabilities.

S - Speak with your support team to gain clarity and perspective about the problem you are facing. Sit with experts in the field who can give you their feedback. Their insight and understanding can help guide you as you move forward to action.

T - Think through the options available. Find a way to escape your environment and get away from the stress. Taking a walk outside can allow you to think creatively about solutions. Have your phone available so you can record any ideas or possible solutions that come to you as you walk.

O - Observe everything involved with the problem. Is the environment causing the issue? Are the people involved helping or hindering a solution? Is there a toxic situation that needs to be addressed? Begin to visualize what your solution would look like and what action steps need to be taken to achieve it.

P - Perform the best action. With the advice of your support team and your own thoughts and observations in place, it is time to take action. Each problem will have a different timeline. Some problems may need a bit of time to enact but, if you are giving the issue your solid attention and you have identified the problem, some of your biggest problems may not take longer than a week to resolve.

In the book of life, the answers aren't in the back.

— CHARLIE BROWN

Creative Solutions

You already know what I am going to say. Creative problem-solving takes practice—a lot of it. Luckily for you, the solving of one problem often introduces the next problem. Or as we like to say at Stop Clowning Around, your next opportunity. You will have plenty of opportunities to exercise your problem-solving muscles.

You will find as you give your full attention to the problem at hand, your brain will do amazing things for you. By wrestling with challenging issues, asking for support, and listening to those around you, more often than not, you will start to come up with creative solutions. Some of them might be silly. Some of them might be impossible. Some of them might not work. (Again, think Dyson! 5,000 prototypes!!!) That is a part of the learning process. Remember that every great invention began with a problem waiting to be solved. In your workplace, that someone could be you!

Everywhere you turn, media is talking about Machine Learning (ML) as a part of Artificial Intelligence (AI). Simply stated, a machine can continually learn as it observes and participates in an environment. With each action it takes, it gets smarter based on the success or failure of its action.

If we were playing chess with a computer using ML, it would make a move. If that move did not work out, the computer would document that in its memory and try a different move the next time. After enough time, this machine would have documented all the probable failures and would know all the correct moves. It would not take much time before this machine would be able to beat even the best chess players in the world.

We, humans, are very intelligent beings with the ability to learn at a similar rate as a computer. The major difference is that we avoid mistakes and failures because our feelings get hurt. Machines have no feelings.

As we learn to embrace learning through failure and not take it personally, we can solve any problem put in front of us.

Practice Creative Problem-solving

- Consume content daily, specifically on areas that could help with problem-solving. Watch seminars. Read books, magazines, and blogs on your problem.

- Journal new ideas and allow yourself to brainstorm and be ok with bad ideas.
- Network with others and plan brainstorming sessions. Allow yourselves to be silly and create funny options. Some great ideas will be found through humor.
- Take an improv class. Train yourself to think on your feet and be more creative on the spot.
- Listen to others. Force yourself to be quiet in conversation to observe both perspectives of involved people. Journal your thoughts on each perspective and what you appreciate about both sides.
- Try new things and be ok with mistakes or failures. It's just learning after all.

Stop clowning around and solve problems creatively!

ESSENTIAL #10: HOPEFUL RESILIENCE

Every day begins with an act of courage and hope: getting out of bed.

— MASON COOLEY

A Different Kind Of Disaster Relief

In November of 2013, tropical Typhoon Haiyan ripped through Southeast Asia. The Philippines were hit with devastating force. With winds up to 195 mph, it left more than four million people homeless, and more than 6,000 who lost their lives. A thousand people went missing. People lost farms and businesses. Countless homes were destroyed, either blown away or buried by the debris that the typhoon carried with it. The lives that these people had so carefully built for themselves would never be the same. Schools and hospitals were damaged or destroyed. The entire nation was in shock. Relief organizations moved in to offer support in this time of unprecedented crisis.[1]

A month later, surrounded by the chaos, with people struggling just to survive, still recovering from injuries and looking for housing, trying to celebrate the Christmas holidays almost seemed like a cruel joke. How was it possible to celebrate or find hope amid such destruction? **It was time to bring in the clowns.**

Clowns Without Borders

In December of 2013, the clowns showed up in the most damaged areas of the Philippines. Donning the red nose is a badge of honor for Clowns Without Borders.[2] They have a mission... resilience through laughter. Gathering groups of children and entire villages with musical parades, bringing laughter, they interrupted the chaos of crisis, and gave people the room to laugh... to connect... and to feel a moment of hope and joy rather than just heartache.

With CWB chapters located in fifteen countries around the world, these small troupes of professional artists volunteer their time to visit areas in crisis. Places like refugee camps, natural disaster zones, and communities shattered by conflict. They know that those children in crisis could be in that situation for years. Recovering from a disaster is a long-term endeavor. Some families live in refugee camps for years, or even decades. After CWB's Christmas mission in 2013, they returned to the Philippines in January 2014 to train the youth in the clowning arts. They need more emissaries of hope to join in spreading the message of resilience to surrounding areas.

Clowns Without Borders is a relief organization that partners with humanitarian relief efforts in tough areas. It was founded in 1993 when a group of kids in Spain raised money to send a clown to visit their refugee pen-pals in Croatia. Their pen-pals, living in a refugee camp, told them that they missed laughter. (Kids know what's up!) Joy is vital to the human spirit. The ability to look to the future with hope can determine the ability to survive a time of crisis.

Naomi Schaefer, the Executive Director of Clowns Without Borders (and a brilliant clown herself!), says that "In long term refugee situations, every resource is scarce. There's always a line. There's always a waiting list whether it's for visas or food or education. Except laughter. There can be enough laughter."[3]

The clowns are making it happen. One group of children at a time. They know that resilience makes space for hope, for laughter, for joy, even in the toughest situations.

Essential #10 – Hopeful Resilience

You can't divorce your human experience from your professional journey. No matter how hard you try to compartmentalize. In crossing the skills gap, you bring your entire self with you. Each skill bleeds into the next. But the most important life skill of all is learning how to dig into hopeful resilience. Your ability to see beyond the crisis or hardship in front of you and the willingness to move forward in hope will determine the scope of your work and life.

> It is really wonderful how much resilience there is in human nature. Let any obstructing cause, no matter what, be removed in any way, even by death, and we fly back to the first principles of hope and enjoyment.
>
> — BRAM STOKER

Not one of us goes through life untouched by hardship. Every human experiences struggle, loss, disappointment, and grief. How we respond to those moments in our lives are very different. How that story unwinds is directly linked to how we view the world and how we navigate it. You will find as you chart your professional course that resilience with a side of hope, will keep you moving in the direction that you want to go, despite hardship and disappointment.

BMC Psychology reports in a study researching the effects of hope and resilience on depression and anxiety, that "resilience and hope are sources of inner strength that contribute to human development and well-being across the lifespan; they can also protect against the impact of negative life events and psychopathology."[4]

In your career and your personal life, you will face difficulties that you did not expect. Things will often not go the way that you plan. You may experience seasons of doubt or drought when it seems like opportunities have dried up, that no matter how hard you try, you are stuck in a place of anxiety or fear. It is critical to know that resilience, just like every other essential, is a skill that can be cultivated and built up, buoying you in life's tough seasons.

In a study conducted by Donald Meichenbaum, Ph.D., Director of the Melissa Institute, the findings share that resilience reflects the ability to[5]:

- bounce back
- beat the odds
- transform one's emotional and physical pain into something "positive"
- evidence a relatively stable trajectory of healthy functioning across time
- move from being a victim to being a "survivor" and even to becoming a "thriver"
- be "stress-hardy"

Those abilities are priceless. Resilience allows us to thrive even in the most difficult situations, using the resources at hand, collaborating with others, and even bringing that sense of hope to others in times of distress. Becoming a "thriver" only happens when you face adversity and overcome it.

Resilience Stories

Take a moment to reflect on the true stories shared in this book. The people who thrived and succeeded in amazing ways all dealt with difficult problems and situations. Not one of them got through their life without disappointment or opposition. Napolean Hill. Frank Bettger. Walt Disney. Ray Goforth. Lijana Wallenda. Albert Einstein. Mabel Hubbard. Steve Jobs. Michael Faraday. James Dyson.

Each story tells a different tale of resilience. Each person rebounded from not one but multiple difficulties. (Some experienced hardship up until the moment of their death!) But unflinchingly, no matter what the circumstance, they chose to believe that the struggle didn't define them... it was a chapter in their story. One that would shape them, but eventually, the page would turn and give way to a better chapter in their future. This belief grounded them and kept them moving them forward with hope.

A Chapter In My Resilience Story

During the early days of my career, I worked for a company that was notorious for going after people that left. They would go after them legally, referring back to a non-compete document that most employees unknowingly signed at the start of employment. I did my legal homework before I left the company to make sure they didn't have a leg to stand on.

The week I started at ADT, the manager who hired me was let go in a large corporate leadership slashing. If that wasn't unsettling enough, a few days later, I received a legal letter stating I was in breach of my non-compete agreement. The terms: I had to quit ADT, or my former company would pursue a court battle. (This was more than a little stressful.)

My new company also got the letter. I'll be honest... I was afraid. I knew that I hadn't had time to develop friendships and cement ties with my new company. Luckily for me, the general manager heard the story and backed me up. In a meeting with the other company leaders, he said, "I think we have bigger pockets than them. Tell them to give it a try if they like." (Whew! I was saved!)

Within the week, I had a call from a detective stating I was accused of killing proprietary data on my old company's network. (Not true!) Yet another detective showed up at our condo declaring that my wife and I had been turned in for a hit and run accident. (When it, rains it pours!) Of course, this was disproved. Our car showed no signs of an accident. But all of this was incredibly stressful. I had to decide how I was going to navigate it. With fear? Or with resilience.

The crazy part was that through all the drama, it felt like the world was caving in a bit. The thing that sustained me was knowing that I wasn't alone (my wife and new company were backing me up). I just needed to keep moving forward. Moving forward with emotional steadiness, engaging in the essentials of relational development, and cohesive collaboration, bringing my authentic self to my work. I also knew that, like many chapters in my past where I had struggled and overcome, this would eventually be resolved, opening the doors to new and challenging opportunities.

Focus On What You Can Control

The hardest part of pain and struggle is the lack of control. It feels like even our best choices are met with uncontrollable factors that do not seem fair. Although my story turned out well, there are many stories that did not turn out as well. In the moment of deepest despair, all seems like it was lost. But using the tool of hindsight, the people with the greatest resilience see how those difficult events contributed to who they ultimately became. The pivot required in their lives was necessary to find their current role of success.

In our moments of great distress, the lack of control seems unbearable. Resilient people have a knack for focusing on what they can control. The only thing we can control is the way we react during difficult times. At some level, we have to trust **if we can control our behaviors and navigate the circumstances effectively, everything else will work out for good.**

You'll never find a better sparring partner than adversity.

— GOLDA MEIR

A New Chapter In The Philippines' Resilience Story: Carigara 2017

Revisiting the Philippines four years after Clowns Without Borders had made their appearance, the hard-hit village of Carigara was still re-building. But something remarkable was taking place.

The people of Carigara had begun to work together in a way they never had before. Yolanda Colbe, the president of the Carigara Small-scale Farmer's Association, said, "Before Haiyan, we didn't care about each other," Colbe said. "It was like, mind your own business, mind your own life. But after Haiyan, that's where we realized — you know, we're all the same. You might have been rich before, but after Haiyan, you don't have anything left."[6]

The devastation of Haiyan had revealed the resilience of the Filipino people. In 2017, they were perfecting working together. Farmers banded together to diversify crops and build out the economy. Townspeople began drilling together, preparing for disaster readiness. Relief organizations supported these efforts in teaching sustainable farming skills. Instead of letting the devastation of Haiyan define them, they were letting it re-define them. They were united and working together. While their country had been devastated, Haiyan didn't crush their spirits. They were becoming people of collaborative strength and hope.

The most beautiful people I've ever known are those who have known trials, have known struggles, have known loss, and have found their way out of the depths.

— ELIZABETH KUBLER-ROSS

A Chapter In Your Resilience Story

You may be reading this book, never having faced a struggle. But more than likely, you are reading this book BECAUSE you have faced struggle. Take a moment to reflect on a recent chapter in your resilience story by answering these questions.

1. How does your struggle define you?
2. How can you let it re-define you?
3. What is the difference between the two?
4. What do you want to learn and take away from this experience?
5. How can you reach out in the middle of your struggle and connect with those around you?

The way that you approach hardship shapes your future. When you see it as a chapter, not the whole story, it leaves room for you to hope, to find joy, and to breathe. Whatever you are facing right now is not the end of your resilience story. It is a moment that will help you redefine who you are on your journey of becoming the person you are meant to be. With resilience, with stick-to-it-iveness, you can turn the page in this chapter. As you overcome adversity, you can become a person of collaborative strength and hope.

Act as if it were impossible to fail.

— DOROTHEA BRANDE

Practice Hopeful Resilience:

- Fail on purpose. Let yourself make mistakes.
- Challenge yourself to conquer small fears, knowing that resilience has your back.
- Listen to podcasts/read books on business founders. Recognize that most failed multiple times before getting it right. Failure is the best educator.

The greatest use of a life is to spend it for something that will outlast it.

— WILLIAM JAMES

Clowning Around Revisited

We've talked a whole lot about not clowning around in this book. But what you should know is that there is one attribute that clowns exhibit in spades: resilience! In every sketch, in every gag, they keep coming back for more. More joy! More laughter! More pie in the face! In the face of insurmountable clown odds? They find a way back in. A workaround. They re-engage. They come at their problem with a different point-of-view or a crazier way to succeed in their ploy of mayhem. With joy and laughter, they are figuring out a way to make it work. And even better? They are inviting others into their joy and struggle along the way.

As you ponder this last essential of hopeful resilience, remember again, that you are the only one who gets to decide what your life, your attitudes, and your behaviors look like. You get to decide, moving forward, if you want to embrace resilience, looking forward with hope. You determine your mindset.

When you choose resilience, you get the chance to bring others with you along that journey. **There is no one else who has the reach that you do or the impact that you do on the people around you.** You can be that emissary of hope and resilience that people need, inspiring those around you on your journey of hope.

With that in mind, flipping my own mantra on its head, I really think you should **START CLOWNING AROUND!** Practice resilience. Lean into laughter. Find moments for joy. And invite the people around you to join you. In your workplace, in your home life, in this amazing journey of crossing the skills gap and becoming the person that you are, embrace all these essentials, and then keep moving forward with hope. In doing that, the possibilities in front of you are endless.

You can know that I will be cheering you on as you go!

Start clowning around and practice hopeful resilience!

NOTES

FOREWORD

1. Simone Stolzoff, "LinkedIn CEO Jeff Weiner says the biggest skills gap in the US is not coding." *Quartz at Work*. Accessed Aug 20, 2020, at https://qz.com/work/1423267/linkedin-ceo-jeff-weiner-the-main-us-skills-gap-is-not-coding/

2. GET DISSATISFIED

1. "Workplace Satisfaction Report: What Workers Want – And What Doesn't Matter," Aerotek, accessed March 3, 2020, https://www.aerotek.com/en/insights/what-workers-want-and-what-does-not-matter.
2. Jonha Revesencio, "Why Happy Employees Are 12% More Productive," Fast Company, July 22, 2015, https://www.fastcompany.com/3048751/happy-employees-are-12-more-productive-at-work.
3. "Job Satisfaction 2018: A Tighter Labor Market Leads to Higher Job Satisfaction | The Conference Board," The Conference Board, accessed March 3, 2020, https://www.conference-board.org/job-satisfaction.

3. DO SOMETHING DIFFERENT

1. Rosabeth Moss Kanter, "Ten Reasons People Resist Change," *Harvard Business Review*, September 25, 2012, https://hbr.org/2012/09/ten-reasons-people-resist-chang.
2. "Who Was Napoleon Hill? Everything You Need to Know," The Famous People, accessed March 3, 2020, https://www.thefamouspeople.com/profiles/napoleon-hill-2424.php.
3. Frank Bettger, "Swipe-Bettger-Article.Pdf," *Syracuse Herald-American*, August 5, 1951, https://www.bensettle.com/Swipe-File/swipe-bettger-article.pdf.

4. BECOME YOUR OWN CHAMPION

1. "Champion - Dictionary Definition," Vocabulary.com, accessed March 3, 2020, https://www.vocabulary.com/dictionary/champion.

2. Dominic Gates, "The Man behind SPEEA's New Tone," The Seattle Times, October 31, 2012, https://www.seattletimes.com/business/the-man-behind-speeas-new-tone/.

3. Danielle Poindexter, "Are You Prepared to Advocate for Yourself at Work?," GovLoop, February 14, 2018, https://www.govloop.com/prepared-advocate-work/.

5. LET YOUR DREAM OF THE FUTURE SHAPE YOUR PRESENT

1. Amanda Garrity, "40 Disney Quotes That'll Inspire You to Live a More Magical Life," Good Housekeeping, April 4, 2019, https://www.goodhousekeeping.com/life/a27032644/disney-quotes/.

2. Amanda Garrity, "40 Disney Quotes That'll Inspire You to Live a More Magical Life," Good Housekeeping, April 4, 2019, https://www.goodhousekeeping.com/life/a27032644/disney-quotes/.

3. "Walt Disney," Biography, accessed March 3, 2020, https://www.biography.com/business-figure/walt-disney.

4. Summer Allen, "How Thinking About the Future Makes Life More Meaningful," Greater Good, accessed March 3, 2020, https://greatergood.berkeley.edu/article/item/how_thinking_about_the_future_makes_life_more_meaningful.

6. FACE YOUR FEAR

1. Rick Porter, "TV Ratings: 'Highwire Live in Times Square' Falls Short of Past Stunts," The Hollywood Reporter, accessed March 3, 2020, https://www.hollywoodreporter.com/live-feed/highwire-live-leads-tv-ratings-sunday-june-23-2019-1220555.

2. Theresa Waldrop, "Flying Wallendas Make History Crossing Times Square 25 Stories in the Air," CBS58, accessed March 3, 2020, https://

www.cbs58.com/news/flying-wallendas-make-history-crossing-times-square-25-stories-in-the-air.

3. Canfield, J. (2004). *The Success Principles*.

4. "Overcoming Fear of Failure: Facing Fears and Moving Forward," accessed March 3, 2020, http://www.mindtools.com/pages/article/fear-of-failure.htm.

5. Angie Angers, "Nik Wallenda and Sister Prep For Emotional NYC Highwire Walk," Spectrum News, accessed March 3, 2020, https://www.baynews9.com/fl/tampa/news/2019/05/29/nik-wallenda-and-sister-prep-for-emotional-nyc-highwire-walk-.

7. CROSSING THE GAP

1. Kelly McCarthy, "Lijana Wallenda Says Times Square High-Wire Stunt Felt like 'Home,'" ABC News, accessed March 3, 2020, https://goodmorningamerica.com/culture/story/lijana-wallenda-times-square-high-wire-stunt-felt-63905164.

2. Will Kenton, "Soft Skills," Investopedia, accessed March 3, 2020, https://www.investopedia.com/terms/s/soft-skills.asp.

3. Jeff Weiner, "Better Together," LinkedIn Talent Connect, accessed March 3, 2020, https://www.talentconnect2020.com/past-session/a-keynote-from-jeff-weiner.

4. Bruce Tulgan, "What Is the Soft Skills Gap?," *Training Industry* (blog), January 22, 2018, https://trainingindustry.com/blog/leadership/what-is-the-soft-skills-gap/.

5. Lisa Roepe, "Why Soft Skills Will Help You Get The Job And The Promotion," Forbes, accessed March 4, 2020, https://www.forbes.com/sites/lisaroepe/2017/08/18/why-soft-skills-will-help-you-get-the-job-and-then-promoted/#423889b954b8.

8. ESSENTIAL #1: AUDACIOUS AUTHENTICITY

1. "Joseph Grimaldi | English Clown and Pantomimist," Encyclopedia Britannica, accessed March 4, 2020, https://www.britannica.com/biography/Joseph-Grimaldi.

2. Robert Mitchell, "Importance of Bringing Your 'Whole Self' to the Workplace," *Harvard Gazette* (blog), April 24, 2018, https://news.harvard.edu/gazette/story/2018/04/importance-of-bringing-your-whole-self-to-the-workplace/.

3. "Personality Types | 16Personalities," accessed March 4, 2020, https://www.16personalities.com/personality-types.

4. "Unlocking Human Potential for over 35 Years Using DISC Theory and Behavioral Analysis," accessed March 4, 2020, https://discinsights.com/about-us.

5. "The I Personality Type Is an Influential Personality from the DISC Profile," *PeopleKeys* (blog), accessed March 4, 2020, https://peoplekeys.com/about-disc/i-style-personality/.

6. Bill George, "The Truth About Authentic Leaders," HBS Working Knowledge, July 6, 2016, http://hbswk.hbs.edu/item/the-truth-about-authentic-leaders.

9. ESSENTIAL #2: EMOTIONAL STEADINESS

1. "Why Does a Circus Have Three Rings? | The Children's Museum of Indianapolis," accessed March 4, 2020, https://www.childrensmuseum.org/blog/why-does-circus-have-three-rings.

2. Alex Shashkevich, "When Are You Most Likely to Catch Other People's…," accessed March 4, 2020, https://greatergood.berkeley.edu/article/item/when_are_you_most_likely_to_catch_other_peoples_emotions.

3. Danielle Boyd, "Workplace Stress," *The American Institute of Stress* (blog), accessed March 4, 2020, https://www.stress.org/workplace-stress.

10. ESSENTIAL #3: AVID CURIOSITY

1. Annabel Acton, "10 Einstein Quotes to Fire Up Your Creativity | Inc.Com," accessed March 4, 2020, https://www.inc.com/annabel-acton/10-einstein-quotes-to-fire-up-your-creativity.html.

2. "A Quote By Henry Kissinger," accessed March 4, 2020, https://www.goodreads.com/quotes/840756-each-success-only-buys-an-admission-ticket-to-a-more.

3. "What Is Neuroplasticity? Brain Plasticity Explained – UK," accessed March 4, 2020, https://brainworksneurotherapy.com/what-neuroplasticity.
4. Carol Dweck, "What Having a 'Growth Mindset' Actually Means," *Harvard Business Review*, January 13, 2016, https://hbr.org/2016/01/what-having-a-growth-mindset-actually-means.

11. ESSENTIAL #4: RELATIONAL DEVELOPMENT

1. Rob Cross, "To Be Happier at Work, Invest More in Your Relationships," *Harvard Business Review*, July 30, 2019, https://hbr.org/2019/07/to-be-happier-at-work-invest-more-in-your-relationships.
2. Jonah Berger, "'Invisible Influence': What Really Shapes Our Decisions," Knowledge@Wharton, accessed March 4, 2020, https://knowledge.wharton.upenn.edu/article/the-hidden-forces-that-shape-behavior/.

12. ESSENTIAL #5: EFFECTIVE COMMUNICATION

1. Marilyn Terrell, "Alexander Graham Bell in Love," National Geographic, accessed March 4, 2020, https://www.nationalgeographic.com/travel/intelligent-travel/2012/02/14/alexander-graham-bell-in-love/.
2. Rebecca Lake, "Listening Statistics: 23 Facts You Need to Hear," CreditDonkey, accessed March 4, 2020, https://www.creditdonkey.com/listening-statistics.html.
3. Allan Pease and Barbara Pease, "'The Definitive Book of Body Language' - The New York Times," The New York Times, accessed March 4, 2020, https://www.nytimes.com/2006/09/24/books/chapters/0924-1st-peas.html.
4. Christopher Klein, "10 Things You May Not Know About Alexander Graham Bell," HISTORY, accessed March 4, 2020, https://www.history.com/news/10-things-you-may-not-know-about-alexander-graham-bell.

13. ESSENTIAL #6: FOCUSED ORGANIZATION

1. Gisela Telis, "Multitasking Splits the Brain," Science | AAAS, April 15, 2020, https://www.sciencemag.org/news/2010/04/multitasking-splits-brain.

2. Susan Weinschenk, "The True Cost Of Multi-Tasking," Psychology Today, accessed March 4, 2020, http://www.psychologytoday.com/blog/brain-wise/201209/the-true-cost-multi-tasking.

3. Dan Schawbel, "Gary Keller: How To Find Your One Thing," Forbes, accessed March 4, 2020, https://www.forbes.com/sites/danschawbel/2013/05/23/gary-keller-how-to-find-your-one-thing/#7a6e9a1a7292.

4. Sam Paul and SWNS, "American Families Barely Spend Quality Time Together," New York Post (blog), March 20, 2018, https://nypost.com/2018/03/20/american-families-barely-spend-quality-time-together/.

5. Ferris Jabr, "Why Your Brain Needs More Downtime," Scientific American, accessed May 8, 2020, https://www.scientificamerican.com/article/mental-downtime/

6. Lauren Moon, "How To Pomodoro Your Way To Long-Lasting Productivity," accessed March 4, 2020, https://blog.trello.com/how-to-pomodoro-your-way-to-productivity.

7. Kat Boogaard, "Take it From Someone Who Hates Productivity Hacks —the Pomodoro Technique Actually Works, The Muse, accessed May 8, 2020, https://www.themuse.com/advice/take-it-from-someone-who-hates-productivity-hacksthe-pomodoro-technique-actually-works

8. "The Pomodoro Technique | What Is The Pomodoro Technique | Focus Booster," accessed March 4, 2020, https://www.focusboosterapp.com/the-pomodoro-technique.

14. ESSENTIAL #7: COHESIVE COLLABORATION

1. Adi Gaskell, "New Study Finds That Collaboration Drives Workplace Performance," Forbes, June 22, 2017, https://www.forbes.com/sites/adigaskell/2017/06/22/new-study-finds-that-collaboration-drives-workplace-performance/#7082c52e3d02.

2. Tracy Middleton, "The Importance of Teamwork (as Proven by Science)," Work Life by Atlassian, May 15, 2019, https://www.atlassian.com/blog/teamwork/the-importance-of-teamwork.

3. Achor, Shawn. *Big Potential: How Transforming the Pursuit of Success Raises Our Achievement, Happiness, and Well-being.* First Edition. New York: Currency, 2018.

4. Martin N. Davidson, *The End of Diversity As We Know It: Why Diversity Efforts Fail and How Leveraging Difference Can Succeed* (Berrett-Koehler Publishers, 2011).

15. ESSENTIAL #8: ENDURING FLEXIBILITY

1. Forrest Wickman, "Why Do We Celebrate With Balloons?," Slate Magazine, December 13, 2011, https://slate.com/human-interest/2011/12/party-balloons-a-history.html.

2. "Fun and Interesting Facts about Balloons," History of Balloons, accessed March 4, 2020, http://www.historyofballoons.com/balloon-facts/interesting-facts-about-balloons/.

3. "Balloon Facts for Kids," accessed March 4, 2020, https://kids.kiddle.co/Balloon.

4. "Change at Work Linked to Employee Stress, Distrust and Intent to Quit, New Survey Finds," https://www.apa.org, accessed March 4, 2020, https://www.apa.org/news/press/releases/2017/05/employee-stress.

5. "DiSC Profile - DiSC Steadiness (S) Profile Overview," accessed March 4, 2020, https://www.discprofile.com/what-is-disc/overview/steadiness/.

6. Gustavo Razzetti, "How to Overcome the Fear of Change | Psychology Today," Psychology Today, accessed March 4, 2020, https://www.psychologytoday.com/us/blog/the-adaptive-mind/201809/how-overcome-the-fear-change.

16. ESSENTIAL #9: CREATIVE PROBLEM-SOLVING

1. Dinah Eng, "How James Dyson Created a $3 Billion Vacuum Empire," Fortune, accessed March 4, 2020, https://fortune.com/2017/09/09/james-dyson-vacuum/.
2. Francesca Levy and Christopher Cannon, "The Bloomberg Job Skills Report 2016," Bloomberg, accessed March 4, 2020, https://www.bloomberg.com/graphics/2016-job-skills-report/.
3. Alex Gray, "The 10 Skills You Need to Thrive in the Fourth Industrial Revolution," World Economic Forum, accessed March 4, 2020, https://www.weforum.org/agenda/2016/01/the-10-skills-you-need-to-thrive-in-the-fourth-industrial-revolution/.
4. Helyn Kim and Kate Mills, "Teaching Problem Solving: Let Students Get 'Stuck' and 'Unstuck,'" Brookings (blog), October 31, 2017, https://www.brookings.edu/blog/education-plus-development/2017/10/31/teaching-problem-solving-let-students-get-stuck-and-unstuck/.

17. ESSENTIAL #10: HOPEFUL RESILIENCE

1. Clare Kim, "Organizations across Nation Aid in Typhoon Recovery Effort | MSNBC," MSNBC, accessed March 4, 2020, http://www.msnbc.com/the-last-word-90.
2. Nicole Loeffler-Gladstone, "A Beacon For Play · Clowns Without Borders USA," Clowns Without Borders USA (blog), April 9, 2019, https://clownswithoutborders.org/a-beacon-for-play/.
3. "Hidden Heroes - Clowns Without Borders Brings Laughter to Conflict Zones Around the World | Facebook," accessed March 4, 2020, https://www.facebook.com/CSSHiddenHeroes/videos/1084521588547380/.
4. Roxanna Morote et al., "Resilience or Hope? Incremental and Convergent Validity of the Resilience Scale for Adults (RSA) and the Herth Hope Scale (HHS) in the Prediction of Anxiety and Depression," BMC Psychology 5 (October 27, 2017), https://doi.org/10.1186/s40359-017-0205-0.
5. Donald Meichenbaum, "RESILIENCE IN THE AFTERMATH OF TRAUMA: WAYS TO BOLSTER RESILIENCE," n.d., 14.

6. Thomas Maresca, "Super Typhoon Haiyan 4 Years Later: Filipinos Still Picking up Pieces," accessed March 4, 2020, https://www.usatoday.com/story/news/world/2017/08/09/super-typhoon-haiyan-4-years-later/525374001/.

ACKNOWLEDGMENTS

To my Lord and Savior, who called me out and chose me to walk according to your ways. You knew me before my time began and placed a high calling on my life to serve others. It is by you and through you that I understand my purpose and get to live it out daily. I praise you for I am fearfully and wonderfully made.

To my amazing wife who literally laid eyes on me the first time while I was a clown and still somehow let me into her heart. You believed in me when no one else did. You loved me when I was struggling to find my way. You never gave up on me even though you often wished that I would stop clowning around. We married young and that has allowed me the blessing of walking each day with you as my best friend. It is with your support that I took each forward step and achieved levels of success we never dreamed of at our start. It is because of you that I finally stopped clowning around.

To my amazing 4 children, Andrew, Olivia, Jaxson, and Caleb. Each one of you consume my heart and inspire me to reach further each day. You keep me grounded to what is important in this life. You teach me something new every day even in the most ordinary moments. I simply want to make you proud and live a legacy for you. I pray this book will help you in your life's journey, but more importantly, inspire you stop clowning around and master your show.

To my collaborative writer, Susanna Foth Aughtmon. You were instrumental in helping me birth this dream. You helped me take an idea and turn it into a literary art that I am extremely proud of. I started this project viewing you as a partner to bring this book to life and end seeing you as a great friend for a lifetime. I am blessed to have added you and your husband to my circle.

To all others that have believed in me and helped me along the way. It is true, the most critical component to one's success is the strength of their relational network. I have too many to thank individually, but most of you know who you are and your influence on my life's journey is evident.

ABOUT THE AUTHOR

Scott Holman is a speaker, trainer, and coach to business professionals aspiring to become influential leaders that find maximum success within the three rings of life (Self, Family, Business). Scott is a leader within a well-known Fortune 1000 company as well as in the security industry as a whole, being recognized in the class of 20 under 40 by Security System News. Additionally, Scott serves as an Executive Director with the John Maxwell team, aligning with a great leadership mentor. Scott uses his experience as a DISC certified behavioral consultant and his personal background in children's ministry to get the best results from his clients by keeping the complex issues simple.

Scott and his wife Michelle have been married for twenty-three years and have four children. Together, they serve others by mentoring prospective adoptive parents and being a voice to advance the progress of diversity and inclusion.

f